interactive
SCIENCE

Red foxes have excellent
senses of hearing, sight, and
smell that help them to hunt.

SAVVAS
LEARNING COMPANY

You are an author!

This is your own special book to keep. You can write all of your science discoveries in your book. That is why you are an author of this book.

Print your name, school, town, and state below. Then write to tell everyone all about you.

My Picture

Name

School

Town

State

All About Me

On The Cover
Red foxes have excellent senses of hearing, sight, and smell that help them to hunt.

SAVVAS
LEARNING COMPANY

ISBN-13: 978-0-328-87138-4
ISBN-10:   0-328-87138-9
18 2022

Program Authors

DON BUCKLEY, M.Sc.
Director of Technology & Innovation,
The School at Columbia University, New York, New York
Don Buckley has transformed learning spaces, textbooks, and media resources so that they work for students and teachers. He has advanced degrees from leading European universities, is a former industrial chemist, published photographer, and former consultant to MOMA's Education Department. He also teaches a graduate course at Columbia Teacher's College in Educational Technology and directs the Technology and Innovation program at the school. He is passionate about travel, architecture, design, change, the future, and innovation.

ZIPPORAH MILLER, M.A.Ed.
Coordinator for K-12 Science Programs, Anne Arundel County Public Schools.
Mrs. Zipporah Miller served as a reviewer during the development of Next Generation Science Standards and provides national training to teachers, administrators, higher education staff and informal science stakeholders on the Next Generation Science Standards. Prior to her appointment in Anne Arundel, Mrs. Miller served as the Associate Executive Director for Professional Development Programs and Conferences at the National Science Teachers Association (NSTA).

MICHAEL J. PADILLA, Ph.D.
Eugene P. Moore School of Education, Clemson University, Clemson, South Carolina
A former middle school teacher and a leader in middle school science education, Dr. Michael Padilla has served as president of the National Science Teachers Association and reviewed the Next Generation Science Standards. He is a former professor of science education at Clemson University. As lead author of the *Science Explorer* series, Dr. Padilla has inspired the team in developing a program that promotes student inquiry and meets the needs of today's students.

KATHRYN THORNTON, Ph.D.
Professor, Mechanical & Aerospace Engineering, University of Virginia, Charlottesville, Virginia
Selected by NASA in May 1984, Dr. Kathryn Thornton is a veteran of four space flights. She has logged more than 975 hours in space, including more than 21 hours of extravehicular activity. As an author on the *Scott Foresman Science* series, Dr. Thornton's enthusiasm for science has inspired teachers around the globe.

MICHAEL E. WYSESSION, Ph.D.
Associate Professor of Earth and Planetary Science, Washington University, St. Louis, Missouri
An author on more than 50 scientific publications, Dr. Wysession was awarded the prestigious Packard Foundation Fellowship and Presidential Faculty Fellowship for his research in geophysics. Dr. Wysession is an expert on Earth's inner structure and has mapped various regions of Earth using seismic tomography. He is known internationally for his work in geoscience education and research, and was an author of the Next Generation Science Standards.

Instructional Design Author

GRANT WIGGINS, Ed.D.
President, Authentic Education, Hopewell, New Jersey
Dr. Wiggins is a co-author with Jay McTighe of *Understanding by Design, 2nd Edition* (ASCD 2005). His approach to instructional design provides teachers with a disciplined way of thinking about curriculum design, assessment, and instruction that moves teaching from covering content to ensuring understanding.
UNDERSTANDING BY DESIGN® and UbD™ are trademarks of ASCD, and are used under license.

Activities Author

KAREN L. OSTLUND, Ph.D.
Past President, National Science Teachers Association, Arlington, Virginia
Dr. Ostlund has over 40 years of experience teaching at the elementary, middle school, and university levels. She was Director of WINGS Online (Welcoming Interns and Novices with Guidance and Support) and the Director of the UTeach/Dell Center for New Teacher Success with the UTeach program in the College of Natural Sciences at the University of Texas at Austin. She also served as Director of the Center for Science Education at the University of Texas at Arlington, as President of the Council of Elementary Science International, and as a member of the Board of Directors of the National Science Teachers Association. As an author of Scott Foresman Science, Dr. Ostlund was instrumental in developing inquiry activities.

ELL Consultant

JIM CUMMINS, Ph.D.
Professor and Canada Research Chair, Curriculum, Teaching and Learning Department at the University of Toronto
Dr. Cummins's research focuses on literacy development in multilingual schools and the role technology plays in learning across the curriculum. *Interactive Science* incorporates research-based principles for integrating language with the teaching of academic content based on Dr. Cummins's work.

Reviewers

Program Consultants

William Brozo, Ph.D.
Professor of Literacy, Graduate School of Education, George Mason University, Fairfax, Virginia.
Dr. Brozo is the author of numerous articles and books on literacy development. He co-authors a column in The Reading Teacher and serves on the editorial review board of the Journal of Adolescent & Adult Literacy.

Kristi Zenchak, M.S.
Biology Instructor, Oakton Community College, Des Plaines, Illinois
Kristi Zenchak helps elementary teachers incorporate science, technology, engineering, and math activities into the classroom. STEM activities that produce viable solutions to real-world problems not only motivate students but also prepare students for future STEM careers. Ms. Zenchak helps elementary teachers understand the basic science concepts, and provides STEM activities that easy are to implement in the classroom.

Content Reviewers

Brad Armosky, M.S.
Texas Advanced Computing Center
University of Texas at Austin
Austin, Texas

Alexander Brands, Ph.D.
Department of Biological Sciences
Lehigh University
Bethlehem, Pennsylvania

Paul Beale, Ph.D.
Department of Physics
University of Colorado
Boulder, Colorado

Joy Branlund, Ph.D.
Department of Earth Science
Southwestern Illinois College
Granite City, Illinois

Constance Brown, Ph.D
Atmospheric Science Program
Geography Department
Indiana University
Bloomington, Indiana

Dana Dudle, Ph.D.
Biology Department
DePauw University
Greencastle, Indiana

Rick Duhrkopf, Ph. D.
Department of Biology
Baylor University
Waco, Texas

Mark Henriksen, Ph.D.
Physics Department
University of Maryland
Baltimore, Maryland

Andrew Hirsch, Ph.D.
Department of Physics
Purdue University
W. Lafayette, Indiana

Linda L. Cronin Jones, Ph.D.
School of Teaching & Learning
University of Florida
Gainesville, Florida

T. Griffith Jones, Ph.D.
College of Education
University of Florida
Gainesville, Florida

Candace Lutzow-Felling, Ph.D.
Director of Education
State Arboretum of Virginia &
Blandy Experimental Farm
Boyce, Virginia

Cortney V. Martin, Ph.D.
Virginia Polytechnic Institute
Blacksburg, Virginia

Sadredin Moosavi, Ph.D.
University of Massachusetts
Dartmouth
Fairhaven, Massachusetts

Klaus Newmann, Ph.D.
Department of Geological Sciences
Ball State University
Muncie, Indiana

Scott M. Rochette, Ph.D.
Department of the Earth Sciences
SUNY College at Brockport
Brockport, New York

Ursula Rosauer Smedly, M.S.
Alcade Science Center
New Mexico State University
Alcade, New Mexico

Frederick W. Taylor, Ph.D.
Jackson School of Geosciences
University of Texas at Austin
Austin, Texas

Chapter 1

Matter

The bubbles in the picture are filled with gas.

SavvasRealize.com

Go online for engaging videos, interactivities, and virtual labs.

Plants and Animals

These fish get what they need in the coral reef.

SavvasRealize.com

Go online for engaging videos, interactivities, and virtual labs.

Chapter 3

Earth's Materials

Plants, water, and rocks are natural resources.

SavvasRealize.com

Go online for engaging videos, interactivities, and virtual labs.

The Nature of Science

Scientists draw conclusions about the things they study.

SavvasRealize.com

Go online for engaging videos, interactivities, and virtual labs.

Technology and Tools

Trains help many people travel long distances.

SavvasRealize.com

Go online for engaging videos, interactivities, and virtual labs.

Untamed Science™

Videos that bring Science to life!

Go to **SavvasRealize.com** to watch exciting Untamed Science videos!

The Untamed Science team has created a unique video for every chapter in this book!

"This is your book. You can write in it!"

interactive SCIENCE

Big Question

At the start of each chapter you will see two questions—
an **Engaging Question** and a **Big Question.**
Just like a scientist, you will predict an answer to the
Engaging Question. Each Big Question will help you
start thinking about the Big Ideas of science. Look for the
symbol throughout the chapter!

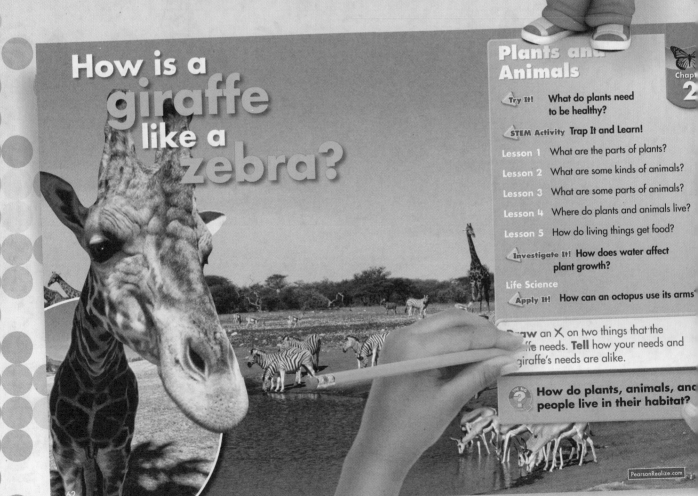

How is a
giraffe
like a
zebra?

Plants and Animals

Chapter 2

Try It! What do plants need
to be healthy?

STEM Activity Trap It and Learn!

Lesson 1 What are the parts of plants?

Lesson 2 What are some kinds of animals?

Lesson 3 What are some parts of animals?

Lesson 4 Where do plants and animals live?

Lesson 5 How do living things get food?

Investigate It! How does water affect
plant growth?

Life Science

Apply It! How can an octopus use its arms

Draw an X on two things that the
giraffe needs. **Tell** how your needs and
giraffe's needs are alike.

How do plants, animals, and
people live in their habitat?

PearsonRealize.com

62

Let's Read Science!

You will see a page like this toward the beginning of each chapter. It will show you how to use a reading skill that will help you understand what you read.

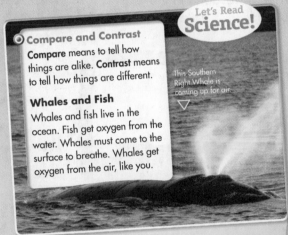

Compare and Contrast

Compare means to tell how things are alike. **Contrast** means to tell how things are different.

Whales and Fish

Whales and fish live in the ocean. Fish get oxygen from the water. Whales must come to the surface to breathe. Whales get oxygen from the air, like you.

Let's Read Science!

This Southern Right Whale is coming up for air.

Practice It!
Compare and **contrast** whales and fish.

Compare	Contrast

PearsonRealize.com   65

Vocabulary Smart Cards

inquiry
observe
tool
conclusion
hypothesis
data

Play a Game!

Cut out the cards.

Work with a partner.

One person puts the cards picture side up.

The other person puts the cards picture side down.

Work together to match each word with its meaning.

199

conclusion / conclusión

inquiry / indagación

hypothesis / hipótesis

observe / observar

data / datos

tool / instrumento

Vocabulary Smart Cards

Go to the end of the chapter and cut out your own set of **Vocabulary Smart Cards.** Draw a picture to learn the word. Play a game with a classmate to practice using the word!

SavvasRealize.com

Go to **SavvasRealize.com** for a variety of digital activities.

"Engage with the page!"

interactive SCIENCE

Envision It!

At the beginning of each lesson, at the top of the page, you will see an **Envision It!** interactivity that gives you the opportunity to circle, draw, write, or respond to the Envision It! question.

Lesson 4
How do some animals grow?

Envision It!

Draw how the pig will look when it is grown.

I will know how some animals grow and change.

Word to Know
nymph

MY PLANET DIARY — Fact or Fiction?

Read Together

All eggs from birds are the same, right? No, eggs can be very different. Think about eggs you get from the store. They are mostly the same size and color. These eggs come from chickens. Ostrich eggs are as big as a grapefruit. They are the biggest eggs in the world. Robin eggs are often blue. Quail eggs can be speckled.

Tell how the ostrich egg and the robin egg are alike and different.

quail egg

robin egg

ostrich egg

72

Animal Life Cycles

Animals have life cycles. A life cycle is the way a living thing grows and changes.

A goat is an animal. A baby goat looks like its parents. The baby goat grows and changes. A grown goat may have young of its own. The life cycle begins again.

Number the goats in the order of their life cycle.

73

MY PLANET DIARY

My Planet Diary will introduce you to amazing scientists, fun facts, and important discoveries in science. They will also help you to overcome common misconceptions about science concepts.

Read See DO!

After reading small chunks of information, stop to check your understanding. The visuals help teach about what you read. Answer questions, underline text, draw pictures, or label models.

Gases

Gas is matter that does not have its own size or shape. Gas takes the size and shape of what it is in. Gas takes up all of the space inside its container. The bubbles in the picture are filled with gas. You know that air is all around you. Air is made of gases that you cannot see.

How are liquids and gases alike?

_____

Where is the gas in this bouncer?

_____

Draw an arrow to the gas in a bubble.

Tell what shape the gas takes.

28

29

Do the math!

Do the math! Tally

You can use tally marks to record information.

This is a tally mark. |

These are 5 tally marks. ⊦⊦⊦⊦⊦

This chart shows how many living things are in the picture.

Living Things	Tally	Total
Tree			1
Bird		
Lizard		

Write tally marks to record how many birds and lizards are in the picture. Then write the totals.

Find one more living thing in the picture. **Record** the information in the chart.

88

Scientists commonly use math as a tool to help them answer science questions. You can practice skills that you are learning in math class right in your *Interactive Science* Student Edition!

Got it?

At the end of each chapter you will have a chance to evaluate your own progress! At this point you can stop or go on to the next chapter.

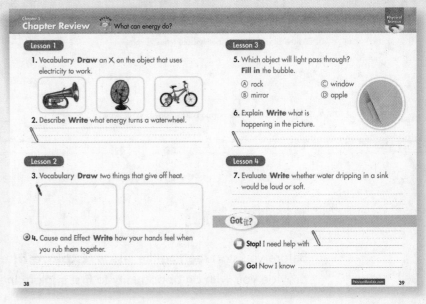

Chapter 1 Chapter Review — What can energy do?

Lesson 1

1. Vocabulary **Draw** an X on the object that uses electricity to work.

2. Describe **Write** what energy turns a waterwheel.

Lesson 2

3. Vocabulary **Draw** two things that give off heat.

4. Cause and Effect **Write** how your hands feel when you rub them together.

Lesson 3

5. Which object will light pass through? **Fill in** the bubble.

Ⓐ rock
Ⓑ mirror
Ⓒ window
Ⓓ apple

6. Explain **Write** what is happening in the picture.

Lesson 4

7. Evaluate **Write** whether water dripping in a sink would be loud or soft.

Got it?

Stop! I need help with _____

Go! Now I know _____

38

39

"Have fun! Be a scientist!"

interactive SCIENCE

Try It!

At the start of every chapter, you will have the chance to do a hands-on inquiry activity. The activity will provide you with experiences that will prepare you for the chapter lessons or may raise a new question in your mind.

Inquiry Try It!

What does light do?

☐ 1. Turn on the light.

☐ 2. Shine it at the plastic wrap. Observe.
Is the light bright?
Is the light dim?
Is there no light?

☐ 3. Repeat with other materials. Record.

Materials
flashlight
cardboard
white paper
plastic wrap
foil   wax paper

Inquiry Skill
After you observe, you can collect data.

Material	Bright Light	Dim Light	No Light

Explain Your Results
4. Observe   What did the light do?

4

Lesson 2
What changes land?

Envision It!

before
This volcano erupted.

after
Tell how the land changed.

UNLOCK I will know some fast and slow ways Earth changes.

Words to Know
weathering
erosion

Inquiry Explore It!

How does Earth's surface move during an earthquake?

☐ 1. Push the blocks together. Slide them past each other. Observe.

☐ 2. Push the blocks together hard. Slide them past each other. Observe.

Materials
2 sandpaper blocks

Explain Your Results
3. Did the blocks move smoothly both times? Explain.

4. Infer   An earthquake happens (fast/slow). Write why.

Changes on Earth

Earth is always changing. Some changes happen fast. A truck digs a hole in the ground. This is an example of a fast change. Other changes are very slow. A river flows through land. The flowing water carries away bits of rock and soil. This changes land slowly.

This truck moves rocks and soil.

Underline a way Earth can change fast.

Write how the truck changes Earth.

The Colorado River makes the Grand Canyon wider and deeper.

PearsonRealize.com

Explore It!

Before you start reading the lesson, **Explore It!** activities provide you with an opportunity to first explore the content!

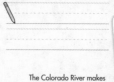
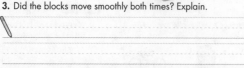

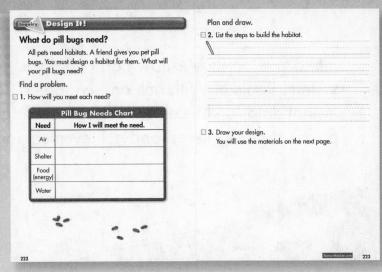

Design It!

The **Design It!** activity has you use the engineering design process to find solutions to problems. By finding a problem and then planning, drawing, and choosing materials, you will make, test, and evaluate a solution for a real world problem. Communicate your evidence through drawings and prototypes and identify ways to make your solution better.

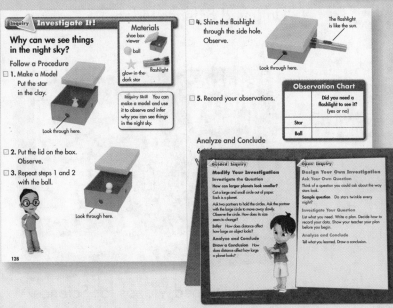

Investigate It!

At the end of every chapter, a Directed Inquiry activity gives you a chance to put together everything you've learned in the chapter. Using the activity card, apply design principles in the Guided version to Modify Your Investigation or the Open version to Develop Your Own Investigation. Whether you need a lot of support from your teacher or you're ready to explore on your own, there are fun hands-on activities that match your interests.

Apply It!

These Open Inquiry activities give you a chance to plan and carry out investigations.

What is Savvas Realize?

Interactive Science is now part of Savvas' brand-new learning management system, Realize! With rich and engaging content, embedded assessment with instant data, and flexible classroom management tools, Realize gives you the power to raise interest and achievement for every student in your classroom.

Engaging Videos

Engage with science topics through videos! Start each chapter with an Untamed Science video.

Savvas Flipped Videos for Science give you another way to learn.

Interactivities and Virtual Labs

Practice science content with engaging online activities.

At **SavvasRealize.com** go online and conduct labs virtually! No goggles and no mess.

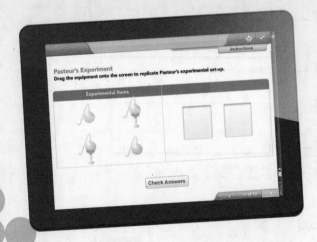

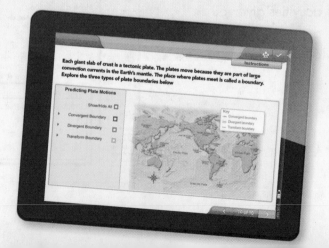

Connect to What You Know

Check what you know at the end of each lesson and chapter.

Get More Practice on skills and content, based on your performance.

Predict your exam readiness with benchmark assessments.

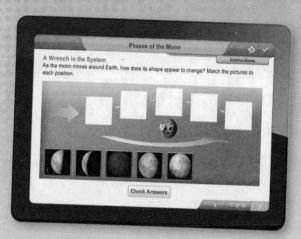

Savvas Realize offers powerful classroom management functionality, including:

Standards-aligned content — search by standard

Powerful Search tools — search by keyword, topic or standards

Customizable curriculum — reorder the table of contents, uploadfiles and media, add links and create custom lessons and assessments

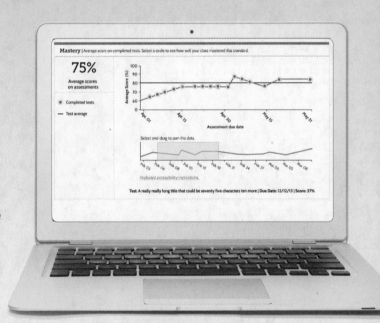

Flexible class management tools — create classes, organize students, and create assignments targeted to students, groups of students, or the entire class.

Tracks student progress — instantly access student and class data that shows standards mastery on assessments, online activity and overall progress.

Track Your Learning Online.

SavvasRealize.com

Describe a Habitat

Your Quest is to create an advertisement. Write why a specific plant or animal should live in certain habitat.

SavvasRealize.com
Go online for all Quest digital interactivities and hands-on labs

How high can they fly?

Matter

Tell what you think makes these balloons fly.

 What is matter?

What affects evaporation?

Materials
2 plastic cups
half full of water

1 lid

marker

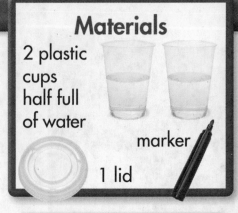

Evaporation is changing a liquid to a gas.

☐ **1.** Put a lid on one cup.

☐ **2.** Draw a line to show the water level.

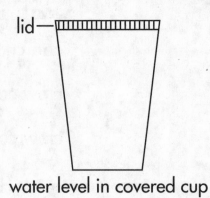

☐ **3. Collect Data**   Each day draw a line to show the water level.

Inquiry Skill You collect data when you record what you observe.

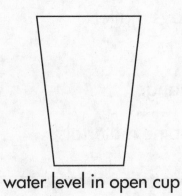

water level in open cup

lid—

water level in covered cup

Explain Your Results

4. Communicate   What happened to the water level in each cup?

_____

_____

_____

_____

5. Explain any differences in group results.

_____

_____

_____

_____

_____

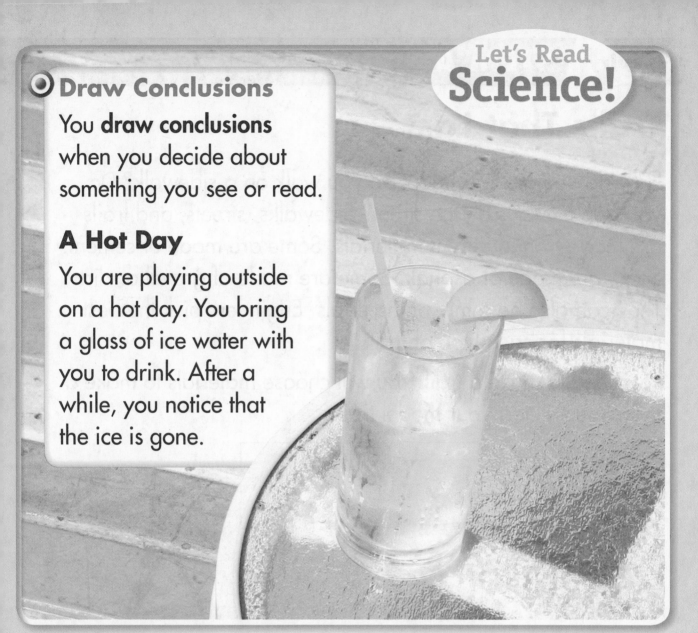

⊙ Draw Conclusions

You **draw conclusions** when you decide about something you see or read.

A Hot Day

You are playing outside on a hot day. You bring a glass of ice water with you to drink. After a while, you notice that the ice is gone.

Practice It!

Write what you think happened to the ice.

I know

It is a hot day.

My conclusion

Trails That Last

How do you get to school? Do you walk on a sidewalk? Do you ride in a bus on the street? Sidewalks, streets, and trails are made from different materials. Some are made of cement. Some are made of asphalt. Some are made of gravel or dirt. They can also be a mix of materials. Engineers pick the best materials for each type of trail.

You need to make a trail. You will choose materials to make a trail. You will test your model trail.

Find a Problem

☐ **1.** What problem do you need to solve?

☐ **2.** How do people use trails and paths?

(blank lined writing space)

☐ **3.** Draw what might happen if a trail is not made from strong materials.

(blank drawing box)

Inquiry STEM Activity

Plan and Draw

☐ **4.** Think about different kinds of surfaces people use. Then fill in the chart. Write how people use the trails. Write what materials the trails are made of.

	Use	Materials
Hiking trail		
Bicycle and walking trails		
Sidewalk		
Street		

☐ **5.** Which materials do you think are best for making a walking or biking trail? Tell why.

☐ **6.** Work as a class. Share ideas about how to test a walking or biking trail. Decide as a class how to test each sample. Write the plan.

Choose Materials

Look at the materials. Think about the materials you will mix to make your sample.

☐ **7.** What could make your design difficult?

_____

_____

_____

_____

☐ **8.** What materials will you use? Why?

_____

_____

_____

_____

_____

_____

☐ **9.** Draw or tell what your sample will look like.

_____

☐ **10.** Pick one material you did not choose. Tell why you will not use that material.

_____

Make and Test

Follow these steps to make your sample. Put a checkmark next to each step as you finish it.

☐ Get an empty cardboard milk carton or juice box.

☐ Ask your teacher to add cement to your carton.

☐ Add the materials you chose.

☐ Use a wooden stick to mix everything together.

☐ Let the mixture dry overnight.

☐ Cut slits around the top of the milk carton.

☐ Start at the slits. Tear the cardboard away from your sample.

☐ **11.** What does your sample look like? Write what you notice.

_____

_____

_____

_____

☐ **12.** Test your sample. Record your results.

Trial	Results
1	
2	
3	

☐ **13.** Look at each group's results. Fill in the chart.

Group	Materials Used	Results
1		
2		
3		
4		
5		

☐ **14.** Work as a class. Decide the best materials. Use those materials to make a new sample. Repeat the test. What happened when you tested the new sample?

_____

_____

_____

Record and Share

☐ **15.** How were the results from the two tests different?

☐ **16.** Was one sample better than the other?
How was it better?

☐ **17.** What made your tests difficult?

_____

_____

_____

_____

☐ **18.** What did you learn about materials?

_____

_____

_____

_____

What are some properties of matter?

Circle the orange that sank.

Inquiry Explore It!

How can you classify matter?

☐ **1. Classify** the objects as metal or nonmetal.

☐ **2.** Find something that is metal and bendable.

Materials

marker

plastic bag

penny

foil

pencil

Explain Your Results

3. Infer Are all metal objects bendable? Explain.

4. What is another way to classify the objects?

Draw one object that you think will float.

Words to Know

matter
property
thermometer

Matter

Everything you see around you is made of matter. **Matter** is anything that takes up space and has mass. Mass is the amount of matter in an object. Objects that have a lot of matter are heavy. The car in the picture is heavy. Objects that do not have a lot of matter are light. The bicycle is light.

Some things you cannot see are made of matter. The air around you has matter.

The cars and the bike are made of matter.

Draw Conclusions **Write** a conclusion about the mass of a car.

I know

A car has a lot of matter.

→

My conclusion

Properties of Matter

Different kinds of matter have different properties. A **property** is something about an object that you can observe with your senses. You can describe matter by telling about its properties. Weight is a property of matter. Weight is how heavy or light something is.

Find an object in your classroom.
Tell its color.
Measure its weight. **Use** a scale.

The tape is sticky.

At-Home Lab

Describe Materials
Observe objects made of paper, metal, plastic, rock, and wood. Record the materials used in each object. Record its texture, color, and shape.

Color and Texture

Color is a property of matter. Matter can be brown, purple, blue, or any other color you can think of.

Texture is a property of matter. Texture is how something feels. Objects can feel smooth or rough. The top of a table is smooth. A dry sponge is rough.

Find a yellow object in the picture. **Tell** about its texture.

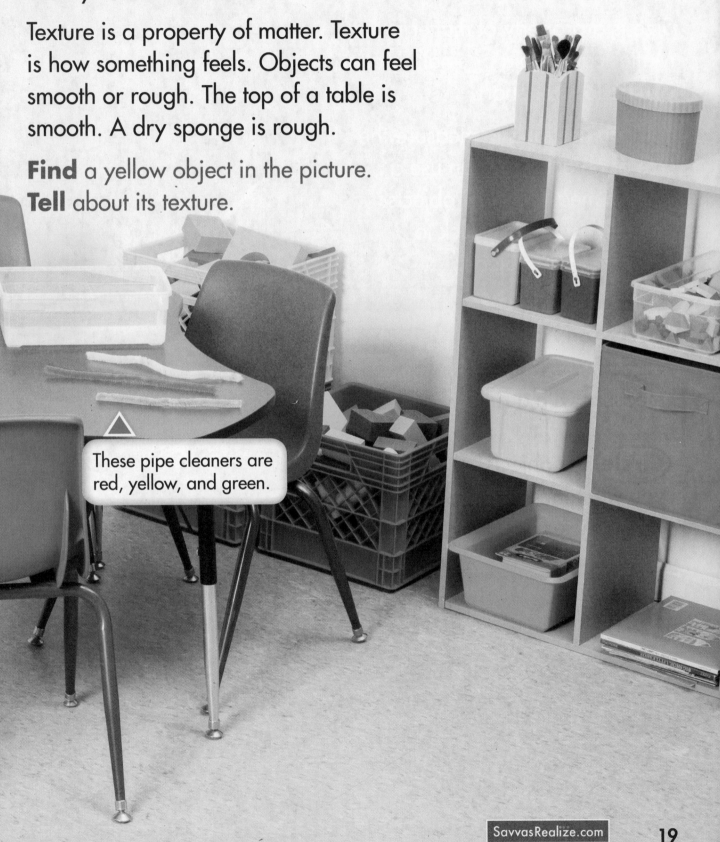

These pipe cleaners are red, yellow, and green.

Shape and Size

Shape is a property of matter. Matter can be different shapes such as round, flat, or square.

Size is a property of matter too. Matter can be big or small. Matter can be long or short.

You can use tools to measure the size of objects. You can use a ruler to measure small objects. You can use a meterstick to measure large objects.

Draw an X on two objects you would measure with a ruler.

ruler

Circle two objects you would measure with a meterstick.

meterstick

Measure the length of the picture of the picnic blanket in centimeters.

_____ cm

Sink or Float

Whether an object sinks or floats is a property of matter.

The golf ball sinks to the bottom of the vase. The table-tennis ball floats at the top of the vase.

Look at the picture of the vase. **Draw** another object that you think will sink.

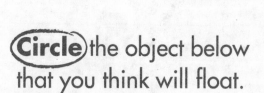

Circle the object below that you think will float.

Temperature

Temperature is a property of matter. It tells how hot or cold something is.

A **thermometer** is a tool that measures temperature. A thermometer can measure the temperature of the air. The red liquid in the thermometer below goes up when it is getting warmer. The red liquid goes down when it is getting colder. The number next to the top of the red liquid is the temperature.

Fill in the thermometer below to show how 5° Celsius (41°F) would look.

Write the difference in temperature between the two thermometers.

This thermometer shows that it is 30° Celsius (86°F).

What are solids, liquids, and gases?

Envision It!

Circle three solids. **Draw** an X on three liquids.

MY PLANET DIARY Did You Know?

Read Together

What makes a thermometer work? It works because of the properties of liquids. A liquid takes up less space when it is cooled. It takes up more space when it is heated.

The liquid inside most thermometers is either alcohol or mercury. The liquid goes up in the tube when it is warmed. It goes down when it is cooled.

It has to be very, very cold for alcohol or mercury to freeze. Water freezes at 32° F. **Write** why water would not work in a thermometer.

UNLOCK THE BIG ?

I will know that matter can be a solid, a liquid, or a gas.

Words to Know

solid
liquid
gas

Solids

Everything around you is made of matter. Three states of matter are solid, liquid, and gas.

A **solid** is matter that keeps its own size and shape. Solids take up space and have weight. Look at the picture. Each object in the box keeps its own size and shape.

Underline three states of matter.

This art box and the objects in it are solids.

Draw one more solid that might go in the art box.

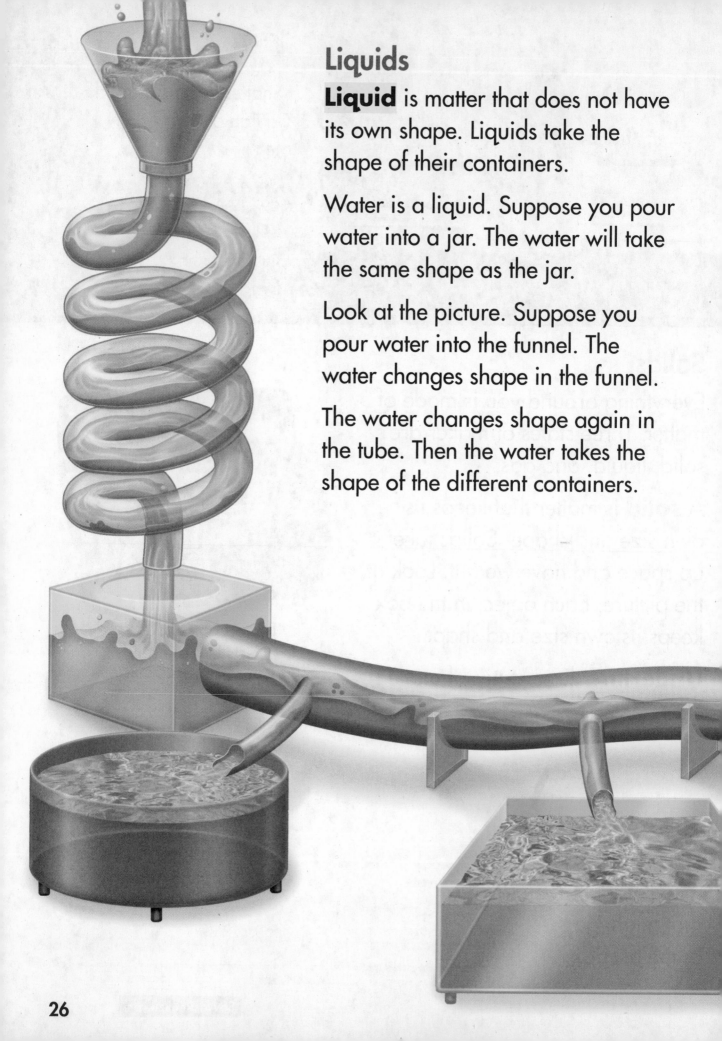

Liquids

Liquid is matter that does not have its own shape. Liquids take the shape of their containers.

Water is a liquid. Suppose you pour water into a jar. The water will take the same shape as the jar.

Look at the picture. Suppose you pour water into the funnel. The water changes shape in the funnel.

The water changes shape again in the tube. Then the water takes the shape of the different containers.

Write how solids and liquids are different.

_____

- - - - - - - - - - -

_____

- - - - - - - - - - -

_____

At-Home Lab

Water and Ice
Put some ice cubes in a bowl. Fill the bowl with water. Tell what happened to the solids. Tell what happened to the liquid.

Look at the picture. **Draw** two shapes the water takes.

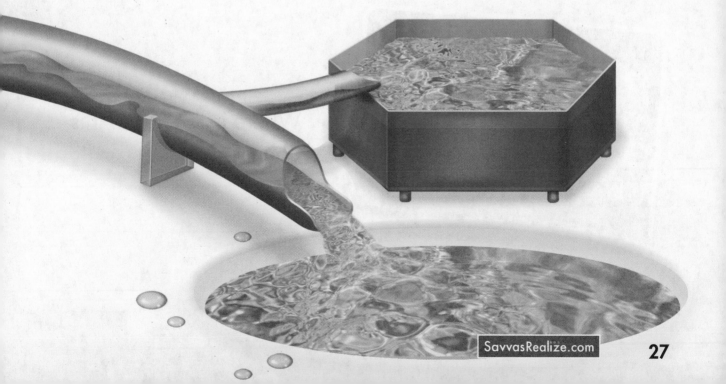

Gases

Gas is matter that does not have its own size or shape. Gas takes the size and shape of what it is in. Gas takes up all of the space inside its container. The bubbles in the picture are filled with gas.

You know that air is all around you. Air is made of gases that you cannot see.

How are liquids and gases alike?

_____

_____

_____

Where is the gas in this bouncer?

_____

_____

Draw an arrow to the gas in a bubble.

Tell what shape the gas takes.

What are some ways matter can change?

Envision It!

Tell how the balloons were changed.

Inquiry **Explore It!**

How can you change clay?

☐ **1.** Make a ball of clay.
Squeeze it. **Record** what happens.

_____
- -

☐ **2.** Add the other clay to the ball. What happens?

_____
_____
_____

Materials

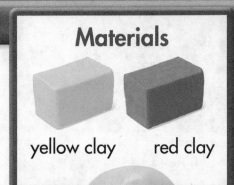

yellow clay   red clay

Explain Your Results

3. Communicate   What properties of the clay changed?

_____
_____
_____

UNLOCK
THE BIG
? I will know that matter can be changed in many ways.

Words to Know
....
physical change
mixture
evaporate

Changing Matter

Matter can be changed. A **physical change** happens when matter changes but does not become a new kind of matter.

You can cut paper with scissors. Cutting causes a physical change. Cutting changes the size and shape of paper. But it is still paper after you cut it.

You can sharpen a pencil to change its size and shape. Sharpening causes a physical change. It is still a pencil after you sharpen it.

What is another physical change you can make to a pencil?

Mold It, Fold It, Tear It, Bend It

Matter can be changed in other ways too. Matter can be molded, folded, torn, and bent.

Different matter changes in different ways. Suppose you pull clay apart. You can put clay back together. Suppose you tear paper. You cannot put paper back together.

Draw the clay and pipe cleaners after they have changed.

Clay can be molded into a new shape.

Paper can be torn to change its size.

Other Ways Matter Can Change

Some changes are not physical changes. Sometimes matter can be changed completely. Baking bread dough in an oven will change it. The dough is changed into something different. Baked bread cannot be changed back into dough. The bread comes out of the oven warm and ready to eat!

The properties of dough are very different from the properties of bread.

Draw Conclusions Look at the picture. **Write** how the dough changed.

_____

_____

_____

_____

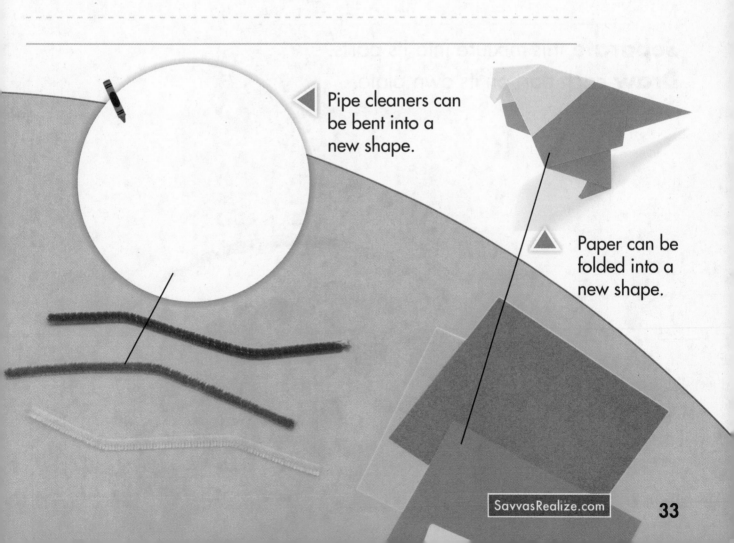

Pipe cleaners can be bent into a new shape.

Paper can be folded into a new shape.

Mix and Separate Matter

You can stir matter together to make a mixture.
A **mixture** is something made up of two
or more kinds of matter. You can separate a
mixture to see its parts.

Look at the fruit salad. It is a mixture of different
kinds of fruit. You can separate the fruit in the
salad. Each piece of fruit will stay the same.

Name another mixture.
Explain how you could separate it.

Separate this mixture into its parts.
Draw each part on its own plate.

Water Mixtures

Some mixtures are made with water. Look at the pictures. One mixture is made with sand and water. One mixture is made with salt and water. Sand and salt are solids.

You can separate these mixtures in different ways. You can let the solid matter sink. You can let the water evaporate. **Evaporate** means to change from a liquid to a gas.

Draw an X on the picture that shows a solid that sank.

Circle the picture that shows evaporation.

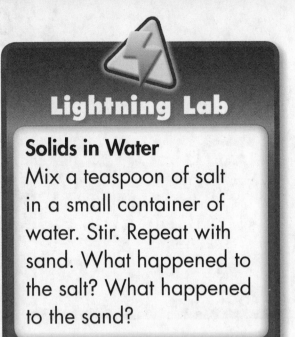

Lightning Lab

Solids in Water

Mix a teaspoon of salt in a small container of water. Stir. Repeat with sand. What happened to the salt? What happened to the sand?

water with sand

water with salt

How can water change?

Envision It!

Tell how the ice is changing.

Inquiry Explore It!

How much water is in each cup?

Materials

crayon

3 plastic measuring cups
(one with colored water)

☐ **1.** There are _____ mL in the first cup.

☐ **2.** Pour the liquid into another cup.
Measure. Record your data.

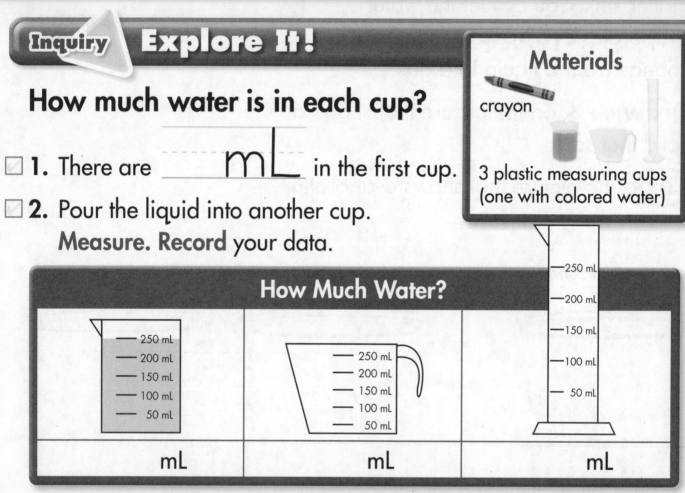

How Much Water?

— 250 mL — 200 mL — 150 mL — 100 mL — 50 mL	— 250 mL — 200 mL — 150 mL — 100 mL — 50 mL	—250 mL —200 mL —150 mL —100 mL — 50 mL
mL	mL	mL

Explain Your Results

3. Observe How did the volume and shape of the water change?

_____

Changing Shape

Matter can be changed. Water is matter. You can change the shape of water.

Suppose you pour a cup of water into a tall, thin container. The shape of the water will change. It looks like there is more liquid. However, the volume of the liquid is the same. **Volume** is the amount of space matter takes up. The volume of a liquid stays the same when it is poured into different kinds of containers.

Look at the pictures. **Tell** what shape the water takes.

The same amount of water was used to fill each of these containers.

Cooling Matter

Cooling can change the state of matter. Water can be a solid, a liquid, or a gas.

Water can change from a liquid to a solid. Suppose the air temperature is very cold. Rain will freeze and change to ice. Ice is a solid.

Water can change from a gas to a liquid too. Have you ever had a cold drink on a hot day? Water vapor in the air touches the cold glass. The water vapor changes from a gas to a liquid. Tiny drops of water form on the glass.

Water on these leaves changed from a liquid to a solid.

Lightning Lab

Effects of Temperature
Mix a teaspoon of sugar in a glass of cold water. Next, mix a teaspoon of sugar in a glass of very warm water. Tell how the temperature of the water affects what happens.

Look at the picture above. How is ice different from water?

_____

_____

_____

_____

_____

_____

_____

Heating Matter

Heating can change the state of matter too. Ice and snow melt when the air warms. Solid water becomes liquid.

Puddles evaporate into the air. The liquid water in the puddles changes to water vapor. Water vapor is a gas.

Suppose the temperature of water is very hot. Water boils and changes to water vapor. Water vapor is inside the bubbles of the boiling water.

Label the water as a solid, a liquid, or a gas. **Tell** about the water in each picture.

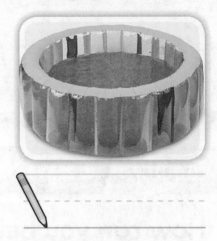

_____

_____

_____

How can you combine materials?

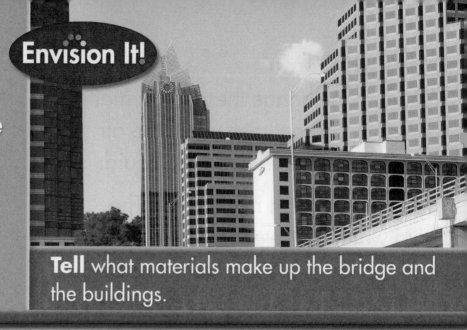

Envision It!

Tell what materials make up the bridge and the buildings.

Inquiry **Explore It!**

How can you build a bridge?

☐ **1.** Plan a design for a bridge that will hold a toy car.

☐ **2.** Choose materials.

☐ **3.** Build the bridge, and put the toy car on it.

Materials

cardboard tubes

straws

heavy paper

tape

clay

toy car

scissors

pencil

posterboard

Explain Your Results

4. Communicate What materials did you use? Tell why.

5. Infer Could you have used just one kind of material? Explain.

UNLOCK THE BIG ? I will know that materials can be combined to make or build things.

Word to Know

combine

Properties of Materials

Materials have many different properties. Materials may be strong. They may be sticky. They may be hard. How you use a material depends on its properties.

Tape is flexible and sticky. You can use tape to seal a box. You can use tape to wrap a gift. The properties of tape make it useful for these jobs.

<u>Underline</u> the properties that make tape useful for wrapping a gift.

The girl is using tape to keep the bag closed.

SavvasRealize.com

41

Combining Materials

You can combine materials that have different properties. You **combine** materials when you put them together. You can use combined materials to make things that you could not make with just one material.

You could not make a kite with just string. You could not make a kite with just paper. You need more than one material to make a kite. You need paper, lightweight cloth, or plastic. You need thread or glue. You need thin wood strips and string. By combining these materials, you can make a kite.

The girl's kite is made of cloth, wood, and string.

Underline the materials you need to make a kite.

A kite is not the only thing you can make with those materials. What else can you make with them? You can make a tent. You can make a toy boat. The same materials can be combined in many different ways.

Have you ever played with building blocks? You can combine the blocks to make an object such as a building. But then you can take it all apart! You can combine the blocks in a different way to make something new.

Look at the building blocks.
Tell what other things you can make with these blocks.

Combined Materials

Some materials are combinations of other materials. Steel is a combination of iron and other materials. Steel is a strong, hard metal, which makes it a good building material. It can be formed into beams, cables, and wire. Steel has other uses too. Some pots and pans are made of steel. Even some works of art are steel.

Steel is one of the materials used to build this museum.

Like steel, concrete is a combination of materials. Cement, sand, gravel, and water make up concrete. Workers pour concrete into forms. The concrete hardens. The hardened concrete is strong.

Name steel things you have seen or used.

An artist made this sculpture out of steel.

Materials in Bridges

Many bridges are made of concrete and steel. Steel cables and beams are part of the bridges. Thick concrete poles help hold up the bridges. The roadways are concrete. Concrete and steel bridges are strong.

Not all bridges are made of steel and concrete. You can find other materials in bridges too. Some footbridges are made of wood. Wood is not the only material in these bridges though. Bolts or nails hold the wooden parts together. Bolts and nails are made of metal.

Look at the photographs of the bridges. **Compare** the bridges. **Tell** how they are alike and different.

This footbridge is in a garden.

This bridge connects two parks.

Building Materials

Bridges are structures. Houses and towers are structures too. A structure is something that is constructed. Many structures have concrete and steel parts. Other materials used in structures are glass, wood, stone, and brick. Each kind of material has its own properties and uses.

Look at these homes. Their windows are glass. The window frames are wood. Some of the outside walls are brick and mortar. Mortar holds the bricks together. These homes could not be built with just one material. They needed a combination of materials.

Look around your home. **Write** a list of materials that are part of the building.

Builders used many different materials when they built these homes.

This tower is in Dallas, Texas.

Materials in Towers

A tower is a very tall building. Towers are also called skyscrapers. You can see many different materials in towers. Look at the tower in the picture. The outside of the tower is mostly glass and concrete. Other towers might have stone or steel walls. Take a look inside the tower. You might see steel, wood, glass, stone, and other materials.

Explain why builders use many materials when building structures.

_____

_____

_____

Lightning Lab

Build a Tower
Collect materials for building a tower. With a partner, plan and build a tall tower. Your tower should be able to stand up on its own. Make a list of the materials you use. Discuss why you had to use more than one material.

How can properties change?

Follow a Procedure

☐ **1.** Put 30 mL of glue in a measuring cup. **Observe** the properties of the glue. **Record.**

Substance Observations

Property	Glue	New Substance
Color		
Texture		
State of Matter (solid, liquid, gas)		

☐ **2.** Add two drops of food coloring.

Be careful! Wear safety goggles.

Materials

measuring cup

safety goggles

spoon

water

borax solution

glue and food coloring

Inquiry Skill
After making an observation you can **record** your data in a chart.

240CC
210CC
180CC
150CC
120CC
90CC
60CC
30CC

1cc = 1 mL

3. Add 15 mL of water to the cup.
Stir the mixture. Observe its properties.

4. Add 15 mL of borax solution.
Stir. Observe what happens.

5. Observe the new substance.
Investigate its properties.
Record your observations.

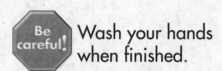 Wash your hands when finished.

Analyze and Conclude

6. Compare the glue and the new substance.
How are the properties different?

_____

_____

_____

_____

7. **Infer** Would the new substance
be a good glue? Explain.

_____

_____

_____

_____

From Sand to Glass

An artist made this glass sculpture. Glass is used in everyday objects such as eyeglasses too. Glass objects can look different. But they all have something in common. They are made from sand.

Glass is made mostly from melted sand. Sand melts at very high temperatures. The melted sand is soft. It hardens into glass when it cools.

Big World

My World

How is hot, melted sand different from glass?

Vocabulary Smart Cards

matter
property
thermometer
solid
liquid
gas
physical
  change
mixture
evaporate
volume
combine

Play a Game!

Cut out the cards.

Work with a partner.

Cover up the words.

Use the pictures to guess the words.

51

solid

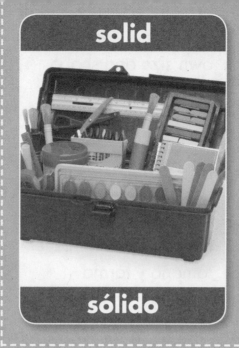

sólido

matter

materia

liquid

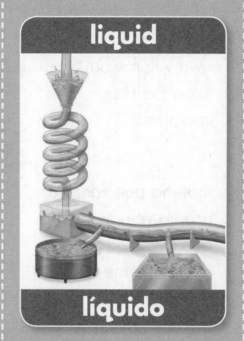

líquido

property

propiedad

gas

gas

thermometer

termómetro

anything that takes up space and has mass

todo lo que ocupa espacio y tiene masa

matter that keeps its own size and shape

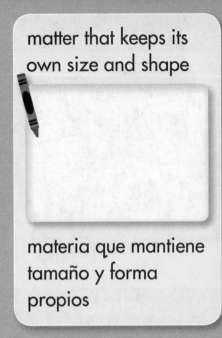

materia que mantiene tamaño y forma propios

something about an object that you can observe with your senses

algo en un objeto que puedes observar con tus sentidos

matter that has its own volume but takes the shape of its container

materia que tiene su propio volumen pero que toma la forma del recipiente que la contiene

a tool that measures temperature

instrumento para medir la temperatura

matter that does not have its own size or shape

materia que no tiene tamaño ni forma propios

 52

volume

volumen

physical change

cambio físico

combine

combinar

mixture

mezcla

evaporate

evaporarse

a change to matter without making it a new kind of matter

un cambio a la materia que no la convierte en una materia nueva

the amount of space matter takes up

cantidad de espacio que ocupa la materia

something made up of two or more kinds of matter

algo formado por varios tipos de materia

to put two or more things together

unir dos o más cosas

to change from a liquid to a gas

cambiar de líquido a gas

Lesson 1

What are some properties of matter?

- Temperature, weight, texture, and sinking or floating are properties of matter.
- You can use a thermometer to measure temperature.

Lesson 2

What are solids, liquids, and gases?

- Solids keep their own shape. Liquids and gases take the shape of their containers.

Lesson 3

What are some ways matter can change?

- Cutting is a physical change.
- You can stir matter to make a mixture.
- Water evaporates when it changes into a gas.

Lesson 4

How can water change?

- Water can be a solid, a liquid, or a gas.
- Volume is the amount of space matter takes up.

Lesson 5

How can you combine materials?

- Materials have many different properties.
- You can combine materials to make different things.

Chapter Review

REVIEW THE BIG ? **What is matter?**

Lesson 1

1. Vocabulary Write two things you know about matter.

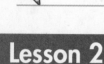

_____

Lesson 2

2. Classify Circle the solids. Draw an X on the liquid.

3. Vocabulary Which state of matter takes up all the space inside its container? **Fill in** the bubble.

Ⓐ solid   © gas

Ⓑ liquid   Ⓓ property

Lesson 3

◉ **4. Draw Conclusions Write** what made the candle melt.

_____

_____

_____

5. Vocabulary **Complete** the sentence.

A _____ is something made up
of two or more kinds of matter.

Lesson 4

6. **Describe** How are water and water vapor different?

_____

_____

_____

Lesson 5

7. **Explain Draw** a bike. What materials are combined to
make a bike?

_____

_____

_____

_____

Got it?

⬜ **Stop!** I need help with _____

_____

▶ **Go!** Now I know _____

Which objects will float?

Materials

objects

water

Inquiry Skill
When you **classify**, you sort things.

Some objects float. Other objects sink.

Ask a question.

Which objects will float?

Make a prediction.

1. Choose an object. Tell what you think.

The _____ will (**float / sink**).

Plan a fair test.

Use all of the objects.
Make predictions before you test.

Be careful! Make sure to clean up spills!

Design your test.

☑ **2.** List your steps.

_____

_____

_____

_____

_____

_____

_____

Do your test.

☑ **3.** Follow your steps.

Collect and record data.

☑ **4.** Fill in the chart.

Tell your conclusion.

5. Classify Which objects float?

_____

6. Which objects sink?

_____

Performance-Based Assessment

Science and Engineering Practices

1. Ask a question or define a problem.
2. Develop and use models.
3. Plan and carry out investigations.
4. Analyze and interpret data.
5. Use math and computational thinking.
6. Construct explanations or design solutions.
7. Engage in argument from evidence.
8. Obtain, evaluate, and communicate information.

Group Objects

- Group objects such as buttons or blocks by the materials they are made of.
- Label the groups. Write a sentence about each group.
- Why did you group the objects this way?
- What is a different way you could group these objects?

Cool a Balloon

- Blow up a balloon.
- Find out if the size of the balloon changes when it is in cold water.
- Write what happens.
- Predict what you think will happen when you take the balloon out of the cold water.
- Test your prediction.
- Write what happens.

Order Objects by Mass

- Choose three objects.

- Predict which object will have the least mass and which will have the most mass.

- Write about your predictions.

- Use a pan balance to test your predictions.

- Were your predictions right?

Make a Presentation

- Gather materials. Make an object such as a mobile.

- Use the same set of materials to make another object that is different from the first.

- Describe the properties of the materials you used. Show how the materials can be combined in different ways.

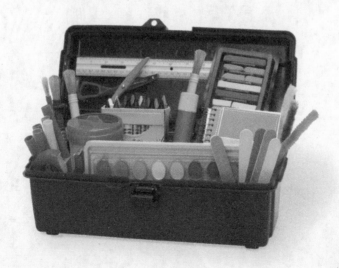

How is a giraffe like a zebra?

Plants and Animals

Draw an X on two things that the giraffe needs. **Tell** how your needs and a giraffe's needs are alike.

 How do plants, animals, and people live in their habitat?

What do plants need to be healthy?

☐ **1.** Put 10 seeds in Cup A.
Put 10 seeds in Cup B.

☐ **2.** Cover the seeds with soil.
Add 4 spoonfuls of water.

Put Cup A in sunlight.
Put Cup B in a dark place.

Add 1 spoonful of water every day.

☐ **3. Observe**   How do the plants look after 3 weeks? Draw what you observe in the cups to the right.

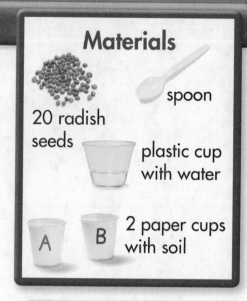

Materials

20 radish seeds

spoon

plastic cup with water

A B   2 paper cups with soil

Inquiry Skill When you collect data, you show what you **observe.**

Be careful! Wash your hands.

Explain Your Results

4. Which plants look healthier?

5. Draw a Conclusion   What is one thing plants need to be healthy?

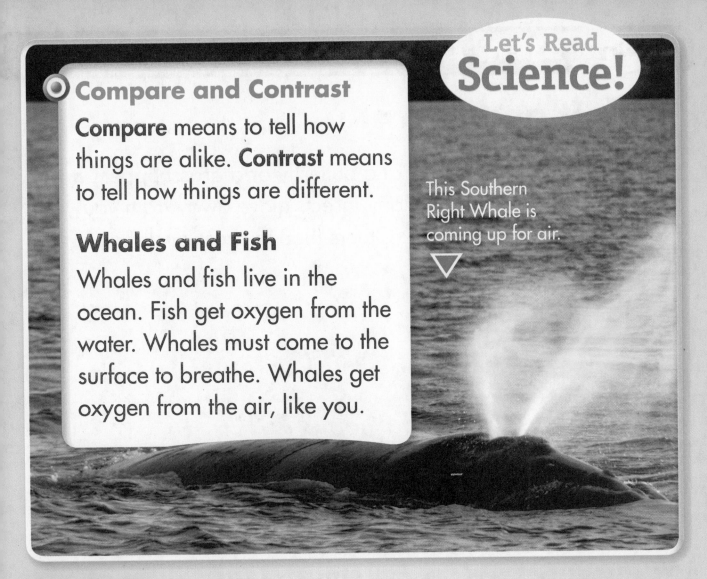

Compare and Contrast

Compare means to tell how things are alike. **Contrast** means to tell how things are different.

Whales and Fish

Whales and fish live in the ocean. Fish get oxygen from the water. Whales must come to the surface to breathe. Whales get oxygen from the air, like you.

This Southern Right Whale is coming up for air.

Practice It!

Compare and **contrast** whales and fish.

Compare

Contrast

Trap It and Learn!

Have you ever tried to look at a butterfly or a grasshopper? It can be hard to see them. Many insects move away from you when you get close to them. Others hide in grass or dirt or leaves.

Scientists use traps to catch and study insects. Sometimes an insect enters a trap because it does not see the trap. Other times an insect enters a trap to get food. A trap must catch an insect without hurting it.

You have to help a scientist catch an insect. Choose an insect to catch. Find out where the insect lives. Find out what the insect eats.

Find a Problem

☐ **1.** What problem do you need to solve?

☐ **2.** Where can you catch an insect? Draw a picture that shows the place.

Plan and Draw

☐ **3.** Look at the pictures of insects. How do insects move?

_____

_____

_____

☐ **4.** Where can you find insects? How can you attract insects?

_____

_____

_____

_____

_____

_____

☐ **5.** What could make your design difficult?

_____

_____

_____

_____

☑ **6.** Think about how insects move, what they eat, and where they live. Use what you know to plan your trap. Draw a picture of the trap you will make.

Choose Materials

Look at the materials. Think about how to use the materials to make an insect trap.

☐ **7.** What materials will you use to make your trap?
Explain why.

_____

_____

_____

_____

_____

_____

_____

☐ **8.** Pick one material you did not choose. Tell why you will not use that material.

_____

_____

_____

_____

☐ **9.** Think about the materials you will use. Do the materials give you new ideas for your design? Draw what your trap will look like. Label the materials in your drawing.

Make and Test

Build your insect trap. Go outside. **Test** your trap.

☐ **10.** Draw your trap as it looks outside. Label all the parts.

☐ **11. Observe** your trap for several minutes. Are insects moving in or out of your trap? Are insects moving around your trap? What do your observations tell you about your design?

_____

_____

_____

_____

_____

_____

☐ **12.** Leave your trap for at least one hour. Return and observe your trap. Draw what you see.

Record and Share

☐ **13.** Did your design work? **Explain.**

_____

_____

_____

_____

_____

_____

☐ **14. Compare** your trap with another trap. How are the traps alike? How are the traps different?

_____

_____

_____

_____

_____

_____

_____

_____

_____

15. How would you redesign your trap? Draw and label the new design. **Explain** how the changes improve your trap.

What are the parts of plants?

Envision It!

Circle the plant part that brings water from the soil to the stem.

my planet diary Did You Know?

Read Together

The objects in the picture are lithops. Lithops are amazing plants that look like stones. They are often called "living stones." They look so much like stones that they fool many animals. The animals think they are stones and not food.

Lithops can live in very hot and dry places because of their shape. They can store a lot of water in their thick leaves.

leaves

Write how the lithops' shape helps them live in hot, dry places.

_____

_____

_____

Words to Know

nutrient

roots

stem

Plant Needs

Plants need water and air to live and grow. Plants need sunlight, space to grow, and nutrients too. A **nutrient** is a food material that living things need to live and grow. Most plants can grow well if they get the right amount of everything they need.

Sequence Look at the picture. The plant is getting water and sunlight. What will happen next?

Many plants get nutrients from soil and water.

Plant Parts

Plants have parts. The parts of a plant help it get what it needs. The parts include roots, a stem, leaves, flowers, and seeds.

Look at the picture.
Circle a part of the plant that makes food.
Describe each part of the plant.

Green leaves take in sunlight and air. They use sunlight, air, water, and nutrients to make food for the plant.

Roots grow down into the soil. Roots hold the plant in the soil. Roots take water and nutrients from the soil to the stem.

The **stem** carries water and nutrients to the leaves. The stem holds up the plant.

Some plants have flowers. Flowers make seeds.

Seeds might grow into new plants.

Draw a plant with flowers. **Label** all of the plant parts.

Flowers contain pollen. Pollen is powdery. Insects and other animals brush against the pollen. It sticks to them. When animals brush against other flowers, the pollen rubs off. It pollinates the flowers. Then the flowers form seeds.

Seed Plants

Most plants are seed plants. Seed plants make seeds and grow from seeds.

Some seed plants have flowers. Many plants with flowers grow fruits. Seeds may grow inside the fruits. The fruits cover and protect the seeds. Fruits and seeds are different shapes and sizes. You can eat the fruit of some seed plants. You can eat a tomato. You cannot eat the fruit of other seed plants. You cannot eat holly berries.

Not all seed plants have flowers. Some seed plants have cones. Seeds grow inside the cones. The cones protect the seeds. Seeds might fall to the ground when the cones open.

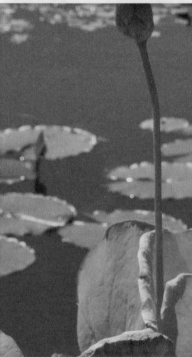

Look at the pictures.
Write how the peach tree and the pine tree are different.

Tell how the water lotus and the peach tree are alike.

80

peach
seed

Peach trees grow flowers. The bottom part of each flower grows into a fruit called a peach. Animals may carry the fruits and their seeds to other places.

water
lotus seeds

The fruit of the water lotus forms the center of the flower.

pine
seeds

Pine trees have cones that protect the seeds growing inside. Animals may carry the cones and seeds to other places.

What are some kinds of animals?

Envision It!

Tell how you could sort these animals into groups.

MY PLANET DIARY

Did You Know?

Read Together

Fish are not the only animals in the ocean. Whales live there too. Whales are not fish. Whales breathe air and feed their babies milk, just like dogs do.

Whales do not look like dogs, though. Whales have side fins called flippers. They have flat tail fins called flukes. Most whales have a fin on their back too. Whales are fast swimmers because they have fins like fish.

Tell how whales and dogs are alike and different.

Word to Know

amphibian

Animal Groups

You can group animals by how they look or act. You can group animals by where they live. You can group animals by their body parts. One group of animals has backbones. Another group does not.

You can group snakes and worms together by how they look. Both have long, thin bodies and no legs. But snakes and worms are not the same inside. Snakes have backbones. Worms do not.

garter snake

earthworm

Compare and Contrast Write how snakes and worms are alike and different.

Compare	Contrast

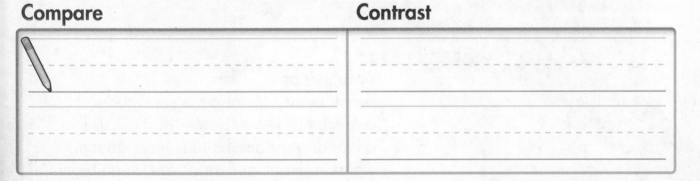

Animals with Backbones

Some animals have backbones. Bones help give the animals shape. Bones help the animals move. Bones help protect some body parts. Backbones help some animals grow very big.

Mammals have backbones. Birds and fish have backbones. Reptiles and amphibians have backbones too. An **amphibian** is an animal that lives part of its life in water and part of its life on land.

Write how mammals, birds, fish, reptiles, and amphibians can be grouped together.

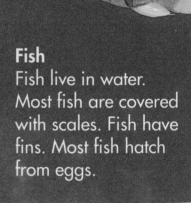

Fish
Fish live in water. Most fish are covered with scales. Fish have fins. Most fish hatch from eggs.

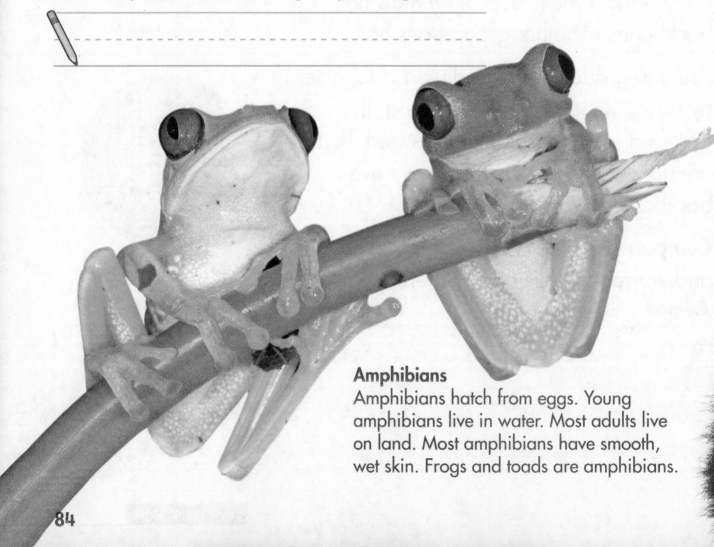

Amphibians
Amphibians hatch from eggs. Young amphibians live in water. Most adults live on land. Most amphibians have smooth, wet skin. Frogs and toads are amphibians.

Birds
Birds have feathers and wings. Birds hatch from eggs. Goldfinches, ducks, and hawks are birds.

Mammals
Mammals usually have hair on their bodies. Young mammals get milk from their mother. Panda bears, dogs, and cats are mammals.

Reptiles
Most reptiles have dry skin and scales. Some reptiles hatch from eggs. Snakes, turtles, and lizards are reptiles.

Draw an ✗ on animals that have scales.

Circle an animal that has hair.

Animals Without Backbones

Most animals do not have bones in their body. Some of these animals have shells or other structures that give them shape.

This beetle is an insect.

Insects are animals that do not have bones. Insects have three body parts. The body parts are the head, the thorax, and the abdomen. Insects have six legs. Antennae help some insects feel, smell, hear, and taste.

Spiders are animals without backbones too. Spiders are not insects. Spiders have eight legs. Spiders spin webs. The webs catch insects. Spiders eat insects. Many spiders feel, smell, hear, and taste with the hair on their feet.

◎ **Compare and Contrast Tell** how insects and spiders are alike and different.

Tell how these spiders are alike and different.

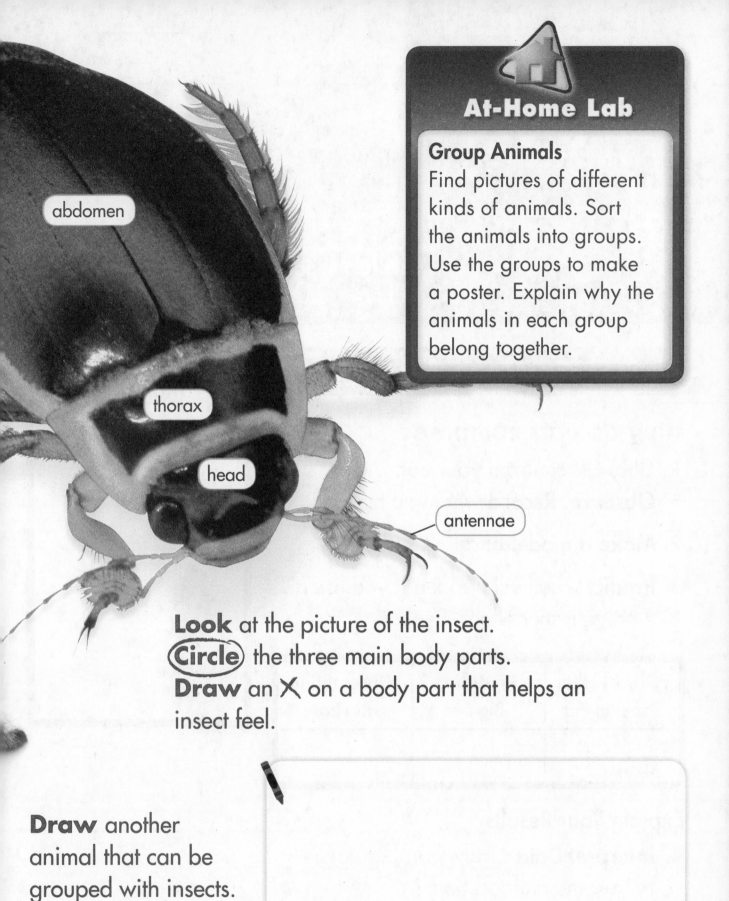

abdomen

thorax

head

antennae

At-Home Lab

Group Animals
Find pictures of different kinds of animals. Sort the animals into groups. Use the groups to make a poster. Explain why the animals in each group belong together.

Look at the picture of the insect.
(Circle) the three main body parts.
Draw an ✕ on a body part that helps an insect feel.

Draw another animal that can be grouped with insects.

What are some parts of animals?

Envision It!

Circle the part this bird uses to get food.
Tell how you know.

Inquiry **Explore It!**

How do ears compare?

☑ **1.** Click 30 cm from your ear.
   Observe. Record what you hear.

☑ **2. Make a model** of an elk's big ear.

☑ **3. Predict** what will happen if you listen
   with your model ear. Repeat.

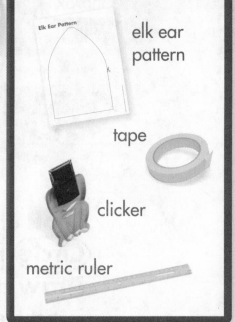

Materials

elk ear pattern

Elk Ear Pattern

tape

clicker

metric ruler

Observation Human Ear	Prediction Big Ear	Observation Big Ear

Explain Your Results

4. Interpret Data How can big ears
help some animals hear?

_____

_____

UNLOCK
THE BIG
?
I will know what animals need. I will know how animals use body parts to meet their needs.

Word to Know

camouflage

Animal Needs

Think of the different kinds of animals in the world. They all have the same needs. A chipmunk has the same needs as a huge whale. It has the same needs as a tiny insect.

Animals need air, water, and food. Animals need shelter. Shelter is a safe place to live and grow. Animals need enough space to live too.

Look at the picture.
Write what need the chipmunk meets.

SavvasRealize.com

89

Animal Body Parts

Animals use their body parts to get what they need. Birds use their beaks to find food. A pelican has a big beak. It scoops up fish with its beak. A woodpecker has a strong, sharp beak. It digs ants and other insects from trees with its beak.

Write why the pelican needs a big beak.

_____

_____

_____

_____

_____

Look at the shape of the pelican's beak. The beak can hold big fish.

A woodpecker pounds holes in trees with its beak. The holes help the bird find insects.

Lightning Lab

Animal Needs

Find a picture of an animal. Glue it to a sheet of paper. Write what the animal eats. Write and draw a picture of how it uses its body parts to get food.

A robin's beak is long and thin. The robin puts its beak into the soil to catch worms.

earthworm

A robin walks or runs on the ground. The robin looks for earthworms to eat.

An earthworm is long and thin. It does not have bones or legs. An earthworm uses its strong muscles to move through the soil.

Write how an earthworm uses its body parts to move.

_____

_____

_____

Tell how a robin uses its body parts to catch earthworms.

Staying Safe

Animals protect themselves in different ways. Some animals have camouflage. **Camouflage** is a color or shape that makes an animal hard to see. Camouflage helps an animal hide from other animals.

Some animals have hard body parts. Some animals have hard shells. They hide in their shells. Some animals have sharp teeth and claws. They use them to bite and scratch. Some animals have sharp spikes or horns. These body parts can protect an animal from getting eaten.

Other animals use poison to stay safe. Some brightly colored frogs have poison in their skin. Animals that want to eat them stay away.

Underline three ways animals protect themselves.

Write how the porcupine fish protects itself.

The tiny porcupine fish can make itself big. Its sharp spines stick out when it is big.

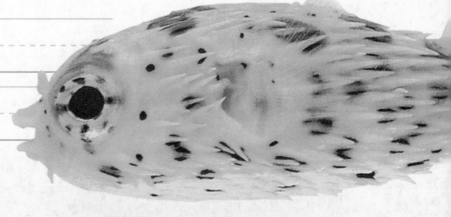

Protection

_____	_____	_____

This crab spider is hard to see. Its color protects it.	Spikes and horns protect this horned lizard.	This lionfish has poison spines.

The fur of this arctic fox changes colors with the seasons.	Pill bugs roll into a ball. They hide in their hard shells.	Coral snakes bite with poison fangs.

Write labels for each column of the chart.

Tell one thing about an arctic fox. **Tell** one thing about a horned lizard.

Lesson 4

Where do plants and animals live?

Draw one animal that you think lives in the rain forest.

Inquiry **Explore It!**

Where can plants live?

☑ **1.** Use a spray bottle. Wet 2 paper leaves.

☑ **2.** Cover one with waxed paper.

☑ **3.** Put both in a sunny place.

☑ **4.** Wait 15 minutes. **Observe.**

Materials

spray bottle with water

paper leaves

waxed paper

The waxed paper covers the paper leaf. Some leaves have a waxy cover too.

Explain Your Results

5. Infer   How might a waxy coat help a leaf?

_____

_____

_____

6. In what type of habitat might waxy leaves be most helpful to a plant?

_____

_____

_____

UNLOCK THE BIG ?

I will know that plants and animals live in habitats that meet their needs.

Word to Know

habitat

Habitats

Living things are found all over Earth. Plants and animals live together in habitats. A **habitat** is the place where a plant or animal lives. Plants and animals live in different kinds of habitats. A habitat can be hot or cold. A habitat can be wet or dry too. Plants and animals can live only in habitats that meet their needs.

This arctic fox lives in the tundra.

Underline where living things can be found.

◎ Picture Clues **Look** at the picture.
Describe where the arctic fox lives.

_____

_____

_____

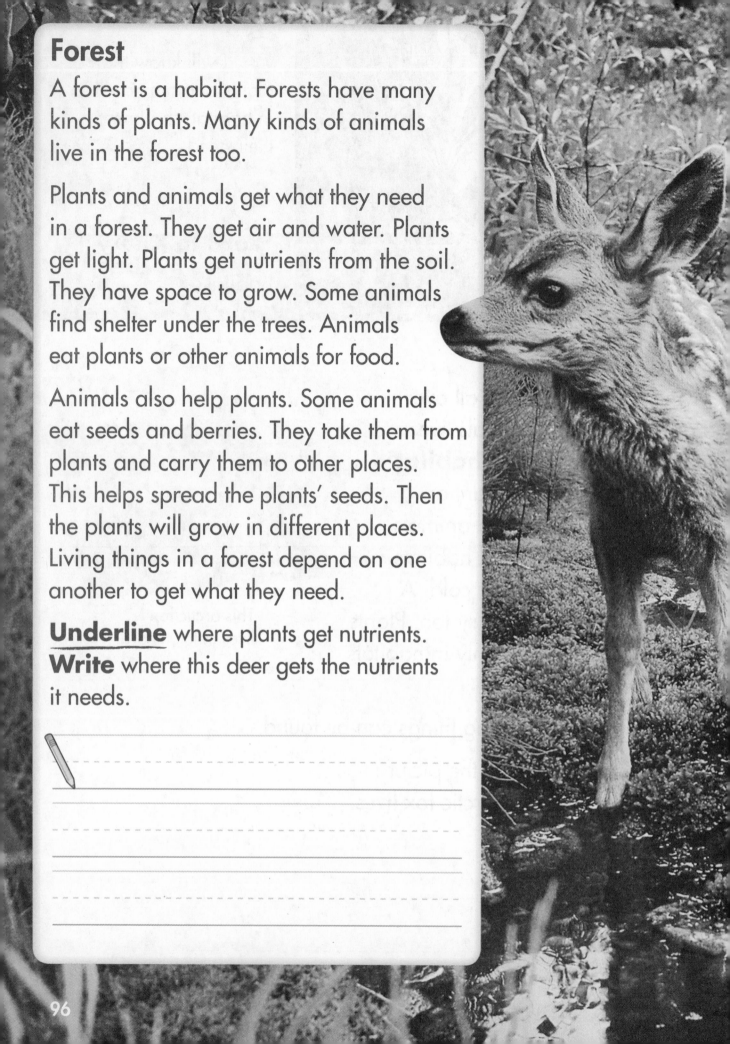

Forest

A forest is a habitat. Forests have many kinds of plants. Many kinds of animals live in the forest too.

Plants and animals get what they need in a forest. They get air and water. Plants get light. Plants get nutrients from the soil. They have space to grow. Some animals find shelter under the trees. Animals eat plants or other animals for food.

Animals also help plants. Some animals eat seeds and berries. They take them from plants and carry them to other places. This helps spread the plants' seeds. Then the plants will grow in different places. Living things in a forest depend on one another to get what they need.

Underline where plants get nutrients.
Write where this deer gets the nutrients it needs.

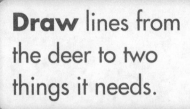

Draw lines from the deer to two things it needs.

This fox uses a log for shelter.

These geese drink water from a pond.

Go Green

Clean Habitats

Living things need air, shelter, and clean water. Tell what happens if the air and water are dirty. Write down three ways to keep habitats clean.

Ocean

An ocean is a habitat. An ocean has salt water. An ocean is large and deep. Many different plants and animals live in the ocean. They get what they need from their habitat. These fish find the food they need in the coral reef.

Write how these fish get what they need.

coral

Desert

Deserts are dry habitats. Some plants and animals can live in the desert. Food and water can be hard to find in the desert.

Cactuses and camels live in some deserts. Cactuses can hold water in their stalks and roots. Fat in its hump helps a camel live in dry places.

Underline how a cactus can live with very little water.

98

Wetland

A wetland is mostly covered with water. Plants that need a lot of water grow in a wetland.

Plants and animals depend on one another to get what they need in a wetland. Animals eat plants or other animals in a wetland. This alligator eats fish that live in the water.

Tell what kinds of plants grow in a wetland.

sloth

Rain Forest

A rain forest is a wet habitat. It gets a lot of rain. Many trees grow tall to get sunlight. Short plants get little or no sunlight.

Many different animals live in the rain forest. Animals find food and shelter in the rain forest. This sloth gets what it needs from the rain forest.

Look at the picture. (Circle) one thing the sloth needs.

How do living things get food?

Envision It!

Draw what you think will eat the corn.

Inquiry Explore It!

What is the order of a food chain?

☐ **1. Make a model** of a food chain.
Color the sun on the plate.
Tape the yarn to the plate.

☐ **2.** Cut apart the cards.
Tape them in order on the yarn.

 Be careful! Be careful with scissors.

Explain Your Results

3. Communicate How did you decide the order of your food chain?

_____

_____

_____

Materials

Food Chain Cards

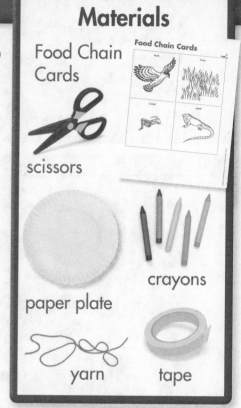

scissors

paper plate

crayons

yarn   tape

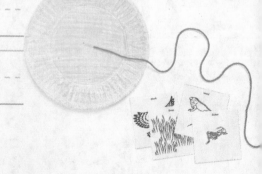

UNLOCK THE BIG ? I will know how plants and animals get food. I will know how a food chain works.

Words to Know

food chain   prey
predator

Energy from Food

All plants and animals need food. Most plants make food using sunlight, water, and air. Plants store this food in their leaves, stems, and other parts. Plants use the energy in the food to live and grow.

Animals cannot make food. They must eat plants or other animals. Animals get energy from the food they eat.

This rabbit uses energy from the plants it eats to live and grow.

◉ **Compare and Contrast Write** how the way plants and animals get food is different.

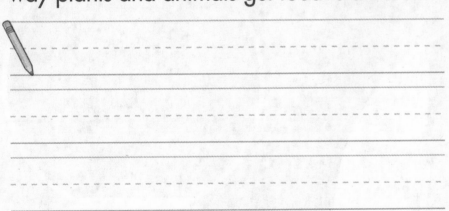

Food Chains

A **food chain** shows how energy passes from one living thing to another. The energy in a food chain comes mostly from the sun. Plants use the sun's energy to make food. Some animals get energy by eating the plants. Other animals eat those animals.

Look at the food chain. Energy passes from sunlight to the hawk through this food chain.

Complete the sentence.
Energy in most food chains begins

with the _____.

Grasses use water, air, and energy from sunlight to make food.

Voles eat grass for energy.

Predator and Prey

All food chains have predators and prey. A **predator** is an animal that catches and eats another animal. **Prey** is an animal that is caught and eaten. Look at the animals in the food chain. The snake and the hawk are predators.

Draw an X on the snake's prey.

(Circle) the hawk's prey.

Hawks eat snakes. Snakes are prey for hawks.

Snakes eat voles. Voles are prey for snakes.

How does water affect plant growth?

Follow a Procedure

☐ **1.** Label one cup **water.**
Add water when the soil feels dry.

☐ **2.** Label the other cup **no water.**
Do not add water.

☐ **3.** **Observe** the plants
daily for 5 days.

Materials

2 bean plants

plastic cup with water

tape

Inquiry Skill
Scientists make careful observations and record them accurately. They use their observations to make **predictions.**

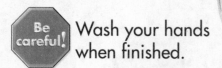 **Be careful!** Wash your hands when finished.

water

no water

☐ **4. Record** your observations below.

Plant Observations		
Day	Water	No Water
Day 1		
Day 2		
Day 3		
Day 4		
Day 5		

Analyze and Conclude

5. Do plants need water? Explain.

- -

_____

6. **Predict** What might happen if you watered the **no water** plant? Test your prediction.

- -

_____

Wildlife Rehabilitator

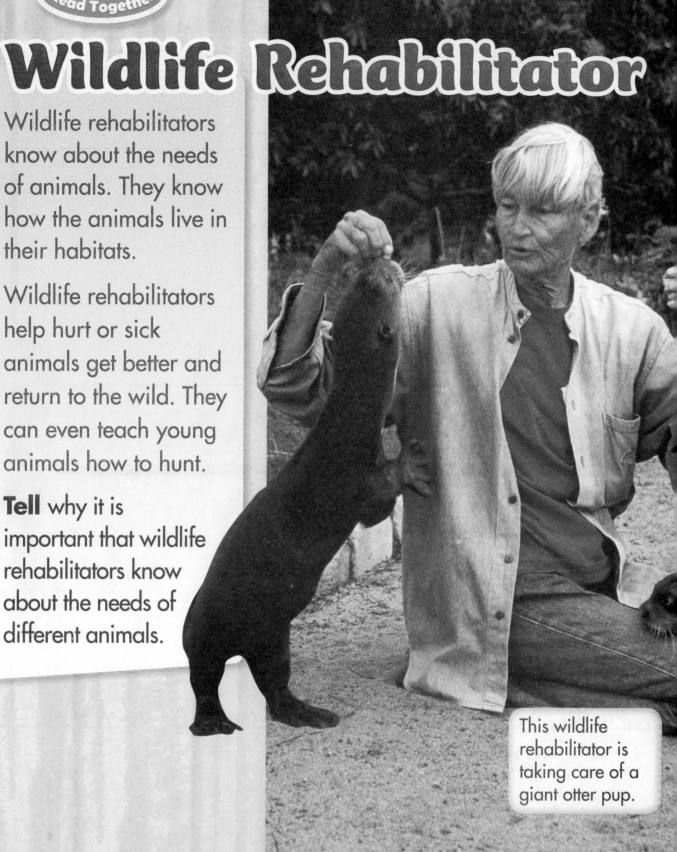

Wildlife rehabilitators know about the needs of animals. They know how the animals live in their habitats.

Wildlife rehabilitators help hurt or sick animals get better and return to the wild. They can even teach young animals how to hunt.

Tell why it is important that wildlife rehabilitators know about the needs of different animals.

This wildlife rehabilitator is taking care of a giant otter pup.

Vocabulary Smart Cards

nutrient
roots
stem
amphibian
camouflage
habitat
food chain
predator
prey

Play a Game!

Cut out the cards.

Work with a partner. Pick a card. Cover up the word.

Look at the picture and guess the word.

amphibian

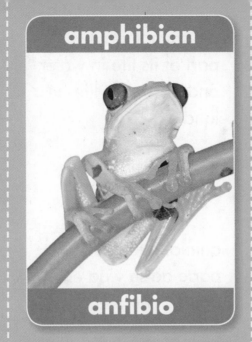

anfibio

nutrient

nutriente

camouflage

camuflaje

roots

raíces

habitat

hábitat

stem

tallo

a material that living things need to live and grow

un material que los seres vivos necesitan para vivir y crecer

an animal that lives part of its life in water and part of its life on land

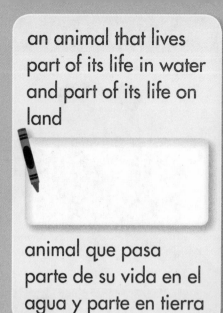

animal que pasa parte de su vida en el agua y parte en tierra

parts of the plant that hold the plant in place and take in water and nutrients

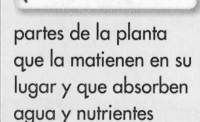

partes de la planta que la matienen en su lugar y que absorben agua y nutrientes

a color or shape that makes an animal hard to see

color o forma que hace que un animal se difícil de ver

part of the plant that carries water and nutrients to the leaves

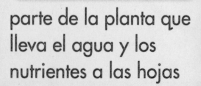

parte de la planta que lleva el agua y los nutrientes a las hojas

a place where a plant or animal lives

un lugar donde vive una planta o un animal

food chain

cadena alimentaria

predator

predador

prey

presa

a model that shows how energy passes from one living thing to another

modelo que muestra cómo se transmite la energía de un ser vivo a otro

an animal that catches and eats another animal

animal que caza y se alimenta de otro animal

an animal that is caught and eaten

animal que es cazado y comido

Study Guide

Life Science

How do plants, animals, and people live in their habitat?

Lesson 1
What are the parts of plants?

- Plants need nutrients to live and grow.
- Seed plants have roots, stems, and leaves.

Lesson 2
What are some parts of animals?

- Mammals, birds, fish, reptiles, amphibians, and insects are different animal groups.

Lesson 3
What are some parts of animals

- Body parts help animals get what they need.
- Some animals use camouflage to stay safe.

Lesson 4
Where do plants and animals live?

- Plants and animals live all around the world.
- A habitat is where a plant or animal lives.

Lesson 5
How do living things get food?

- Most food chains start with the sun.
- Predators catch and eat prey.

SavvasRealize.com

Chapter Review

How do plants, animals, and people live in their habitat?

Lesson 1

1. Categorize Label the parts of the plant.

Lesson 2

◉ **2. Compare and Contrast Write** one way that a bird and a fish are different.

_____

- - - - - - - - - - - - - - - - - - -

_____

- - - - - - - - - - - - - - - - - - -

_____

3. Classify A dog, a mouse, and a bear belong to what animal group? **Fill in** the bubble.

Ⓐ amphibian   Ⓒ reptile
Ⓑ mammal   Ⓓ insect

Lesson 3

4. Vocabulary Complete the sentence.
A color or shape that makes an animal hard to see is called

_____

- - - - - - - - - - - - - - - - - - -

_____ .

Lesson 4

5. Identify **Draw** one animal that lives in a forest habitat and one animal that lives in an ocean habitat.

forest	ocean

Lesson 5

6. Apply (Circle) the predator in the food chain. **Draw** an X on the prey.

7. Explain **Write** how plants and animals get food.

_____

_____

_____

Got it?

⬜ **Stop!** I need help with _____

_____

▶ **Go!** Now I know _____

How can an octopus use its arms?

Materials

paper fish
in plastic jar
with lid

8 suction cups

An octopus has suction cups on its 8 arms. It can use its arms to pick things up. The octopus can use its arms to open a jar and get a fish that is inside.

Ask a question.

How can an octopus use its arms to open a jar? **Use a model** to find out.

Make a prediction.

1. How many suction cups will you need to open a jar? Tell what you think.

I will need _____ suction cups.

Plan a fair test.

Use suction cups of the same size.

Inquiry Skill
You **control variables** when you change only one thing in your test.

Design your test.

☑ **2.** List your steps.

_____

_____

_____

_____

_____

_____

_____

Do your test.

☑ **3.** Follow your steps.

Collect and record data.

☑ **4.** Fill in the chart.

Tell your conclusion.

5. How many suction cups did you need to open the jar?

_____

_____

_____

6. Communicate How did you use the suction cups to open the jar?

_____

_____

_____

Science and Engineering Practices

1. Ask a question or define a problem.
2. Develop and use models.
3. Plan and carry out investigations.
4. Analyze and interpret data.
5. Use math and computational thinking.
6. Construct explanations or design solutions.
7. Engage in argument from evidence.
8. Obtain, evaluate, and communicate information.

Put On a Play

- Pretend to be an animal or plant.
- Act out things about your animal or plant and its habitat.
- Have your classmates guess what you are.

Light and Seeds

- Plant seeds in two pots.
- Provide one pot with more light.
- Observe the plants as they grow.
- Draw and record the growth of each plant.

Make Observations

- Choose a plant or animal.
- Find a photograph of the plant or animal in a book or online.
- Write down what the plant or animal looks like.
- Draw the plant or animal and label its parts.

Write a Song

- Choose a habitat.
- Write a song about the habitat you chose.
- Include many different plants and animals that live in the habitat.
- Give your song a name and sing it to the class.

When have you seen rocks so red?

118

Earth's Materials

Tell how you think these rocks became this shape.

What is Earth made of?

How much water and land are on Earth?

Materials

inflatable globe

☐ 1. **Observe**   Find water and land on the globe.

☐ 2. Toss the globe.

☐ 3. Catch the globe.

☐ 4. **Collect Data**   Is the tip of your finger on water or land? Put a mark in the chart.

Inquiry Skill
You **interpret data** when you use your chart to answer a question.

Water	Land

☐ 5. Repeat the steps 9 more times.

Explain Your Results

6. **Interpret Data**   Use your chart to answer the question. Is there more water or land on Earth? Explain.

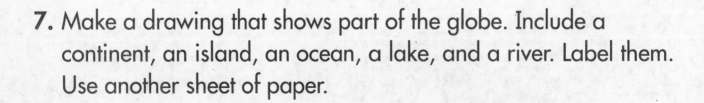

7. Make a drawing that shows part of the globe. Include a continent, an island, an ocean, a lake, and a river. Label them. Use another sheet of paper.

⊙ Compare and Contrast

You **compare** when you tell how things are alike. You **contrast** when you tell how things are different.

Mountains

Mountains are very high. The Rocky Mountains are rough. The Appalachian Mountains are not. The Rocky Mountains are higher than the Appalachian Mountains.

Appalachian Mountains

Rocky Mountains

Practice It!

Write how the mountains are alike and different.

Compare	Contrast

How Can You Make Recycled Paper?

Look at the couch! What a mess! Old newspapers and magazines cover it. Where are you going to sit? What are you going to do with all of the papers? You could recycle the papers. You could make new paper out of old paper!

Find a Problem

☑ **1.** What problem do you need to solve?

_____

_____

_____

_____

_____

☑ **2.** Look at the paper samples. How are they alike?

_____

_____

_____

☑ **3.** How are they different?

_____

_____

_____

☑ **4.** Can you tell which are recycled? How?

_____

_____

_____

Plan and Draw

☐ **5.** Read the directions below. Circle what will you do to recycle paper.

- Cut paper into **(little / big)** pieces.

- Put pieces in a bowl. Add water. Let soak for 1 hour.

- Mix paper and water into mush.

- Add **(one / two)** spoonfuls of starch and stir.

- Put the screen on newspaper.

- **(Pile / Spread)** the mush on the screen. Cover with plastic wrap. Roll dowel over the wrap.

- Remove the wrap.

- Let the mush dry for **(two / three)** days. Peel your paper off the screen.

- Draw on your recycled paper.

☐ **6.** Look at your plan. What can make it hard to recycle paper?

_____
_____
_____
_____
_____
_____

☐ **7. Describe** how your want your paper to feel. Will it be easy to write on?

_____
_____
_____
_____

Choose Materials

☐ **8.** Think about how to make recycled paper. Circle the materials you will use.

Possible Materials

9. What could make your design difficult?

_____

_____

_____

_____

10. Pick one material you will not use. Write why you will not use that material.

_____

_____

_____

_____

Make and Test

☐ **11.** Make your recycled paper. Write the name of your favorite book below.

_____
- -
_____
- -
_____

☐ **12.** Glue or tape a piece of your recycled paper below. Then write the name of your favorite book on the recycled paper.

☐ 13. How are the two papers alike?

☐ 14. How are the papers different?

Record and Share

☐ **15.** Make a rubbing of your recycled paper below.

☐ **16.** Use a hand lens. Look at your recycled paper. **Describe** what you see.

Compare your paper with paper from another team.

☐ **17.** How are the papers alike?

☐ **18.** How are the papers different?

☐ **19.** How will you change your plan?

What are some kinds of land and water?

Envision It!

Tell what kinds of land and water you see.

MY PLANET DIARY

Connections

A chain of mountains is called a mountain range. The Rocky Mountains form the longest mountain range in North America. Only the Andes Mountains in South America form a longer mountain range.

These are not the longest mountain ranges on Earth, though. The longest mountain range is under the ocean! It is four times longer than the Rockies, Andes, and Himalayas put together.

Tell what you think the land under the ocean looks like.

Rocky Mountains

Words to Know

landform
glacier

Land and Water

What is Earth's surface like? Over two-thirds of Earth's surface is covered by water. Most of this water is in the ocean. Soil and plants cover much of the rest of Earth's surface. Rock is found beneath the water, soil, and plants.

○ **Main Idea and Details**
Describe what covers most of Earth's surface.

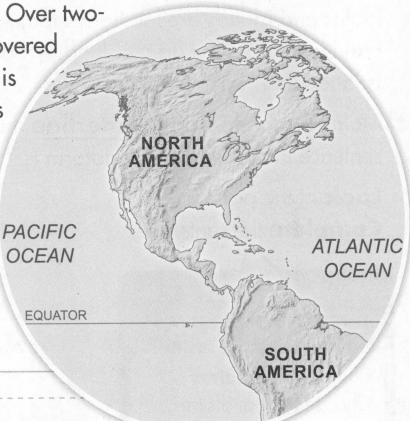

NORTH AMERICA

PACIFIC OCEAN

ATLANTIC OCEAN

EQUATOR

SOUTH AMERICA

Landforms

Earth's surface has many different landforms. A **landform** is a natural feature on Earth. Landforms are different sizes and shapes.

Mountains, hills, and valleys are landforms. Mountains and hills are raised parts of Earth's surface. A mountain is very high and large. A hill is not as high as a mountain. A valley is the low land between mountains or hills.

Plains and islands are landforms too. A plain is a large, flat area of land. An island is land that is surrounded by water.

◎ **Main Idea and Details** **Underline** the sentence that tells what a landform is.

Look at the pictures.
Complete the sentences.

At-Home Lab

Compare Landforms
Choose two landforms. Draw a picture of each landform. Write one way the landforms are alike. Write one way the landforms are different.

A mountain is very _____ .

Draw an ✗ on a hill.
(**Circle**) a valley.

A plain is a _____
_ _
_____ area of land.

_____
_ _ _ _ _ _ _ _ _ _ _ _ _ _ _ _
_____ surrounds an island.

The Ocean

Earth has different bodies of water. The ocean is the largest body of water. It covers most of Earth. The ocean has different parts. The Pacific Ocean is one part. The Atlantic Ocean is another part. All of the parts of the ocean are connected.

Ocean water is salty. People cannot drink salt water.

Tell why you think people cannot drink ocean water.

Lakes and Ponds

Lakes are much smaller than the ocean. Ponds are much smaller than lakes. Lakes and ponds form when water fills low places on land.

Most lakes and ponds are fresh water. People can drink fresh water.

Complete the sentence.
A lake forms when water fills

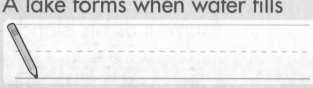

136

Rivers and Streams

Rivers and streams form when water runs downhill. Small streams join together to form rivers. Most rivers flow into lakes or into the ocean. Most rivers and streams are fresh water.

Complete the sentence.
A river forms when water runs

Glaciers

Glaciers form in very cold places. A **glacier** is a large body of moving ice. Glaciers move very slowly. Most of Earth's fresh water is frozen into glaciers. People cannot drink the frozen water.

Write one way that glaciers are like rivers and streams.

What changes land?

before

This volcano erupted.

Inquiry Explore It!

How does Earth's surface move during an earthquake?

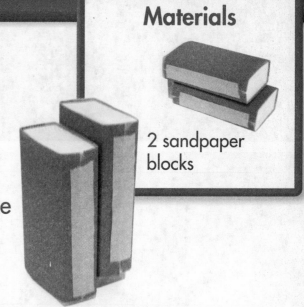

Materials

2 sandpaper blocks

☑ **1.** Push the blocks together. Slide them past each other. **Observe.**

☑ **2.** Push the blocks together hard. Slide them past each other. **Observe.**

Explain Your Results

3. Did the blocks move smoothly both times? Explain.

_____

_____

_____

4. Infer An earthquake happens (**fast/slow**). Write why.

_____

_____

_____

after

Tell how the land changed.

I will know some fast and slow ways Earth changes.

Words to Know

weathering

erosion

Changes on Earth

Earth is always changing. Some changes happen fast. A truck digs a hole in the ground. This is an example of a fast change. Other changes are very slow. A river flows through land. The flowing water carries away bits of rock and soil. This changes land slowly.

This truck moves rocks and soil.

Underline a way Earth can change fast.

Write how the truck changes Earth.

The Colorado River makes the Grand Canyon wider and deeper.

Earthquakes and Volcanoes

Earthquakes happen fast. An earthquake can cause land to crack. Buildings and roads can be damaged. Volcanoes cause fast changes too. Volcanoes can erupt. This sends gas, ash, and other materials into the air. Rock and ash from a volcano can cover land.

earthquake

volcano

⊚ **Compare and Contrast Write** how earthquakes and volcanoes are alike.

Weathering and Erosion

Weathering and erosion change land slowly. **Weathering** is when water, ice, or wind breaks down rocks into small pieces. **Erosion** is when wind, water, or other causes move rocks and soil. Weathering and erosion can take a long time!

weathering

erosion

Circle what causes weathering.

Underline what causes erosion.

Write one change to land that happens fast and one that happens slowly.

_____

_____

_____

Lightning Lab

Erosion
Pour sand into one end of a pan. Raise that end. Slowly pour water over the sand. Observe where the sand goes. Record what you observe.

Write a caption telling what might have caused this rock to break apart.

Water Changes the Land

Water causes weathering in some rocks. The rocks get weaker and break apart.

Water causes weathering when it freezes. Water can get into cracks in rocks. When water freezes, it grows larger. The ice pushes against the sides of the cracks. Over the years, the rocks break apart.

Water can carry weathered material to other places. This is erosion by water. Rain can carry away soil from farms. Waves cause erosion along the shore. Rivers carry bits of rock from one place to another.

Glaciers can also cause erosion. As a glacier moves slowly, it wears away bits of rock and soil and carries them off.

Draw arrows to show which way you think the ocean waves moved sand to form this beach.

Other Causes of Erosion

Erosion by wind is common in dry regions, such as deserts. Wind can carry sand and soil to other places. Few tall plants grow in deserts. This means there is little to stop the sand and soil from blowing around.

Wind can also weather rocks. Wind blows sand and soil against rocks. Tiny bits break off. The rocks slowly change.

Gravity also causes erosion. Gravity pulls rocks and soil downhill. The material moves slowly if the slope is gentle. It can move quickly on steep slopes. A mudflow is the quick movement of very wet soil. A rockslide is the quick movement of rocks down a slope.

Living things can cause erosion too. For example, squirrels make tunnels in the ground. Water and air move into the tunnels and cause erosion.

Tell how wind erosion might have shaped this rock.

Gravity pulls loose rock and soil downhill in a rockslide.

What is a fossil?

Draw a line from the fossil to its label.

Inquiry **Explore It!**

What can a fossil show?

☐ **1. Make a Model**
Press your hand into the plaster.

Materials

safety goggles

plate with plaster of Paris

paper towels

☐ **2.** After 60 seconds, remove your hand.

Explain Your Results

3. Draw a Conclusion Look at your **model** fossil. What can you tell about your hand?

Be careful! Wear safety goggles. Wipe your hands when finished. Use a paper towel. Then, wash your hands.

leaf   fish   lizard

Words to Know

fossil

extinct

Fossils

A **fossil** is a print or part of a plant or animal that lived long ago. Some fossils are shapes left in rocks. Some are very old bones or teeth. Very old shells and wood can be fossils too.

Dragonflies lived on Earth long ago. Look at the dragonfly fossil. The dragonfly fossil looks like dragonflies that live today.

Tell what fossils can be.

Write the kind of fossil the dragonfly is.

dragonfly fossil

A lizard dies.

How Fossils Form

Look at the pictures of the lizard. The pictures show how some fossils form. The lizard dies. Layers of mud and sand cover the lizard. These layers turn to rock after a long time. What is left of the lizard turns to rock too. A print of the lizard is left in the rock.

Write a caption for the second picture. **Complete** the last picture caption.

The layers turn to rock. This lizard has become a

_____

At-Home Lab

Make a Fossil
Find a large leaf. Use a crayon and white paper to make a rubbing. Tell about your fossil.

What Fossils Show

Fossils show the size and shape of things that lived long ago. Scientists study fossils to see how plants and animals change over time.

Some fossils are of extinct plants and animals. An **extinct** plant or animal no longer lives on Earth. Scientists study fossils for clues about these plants and animals.

Fossils can help scientists learn how Earth has changed slowly over time. Sometimes scientists find fish fossils in places without water. This tells them that the place once had water.

<u>**Underline**</u> three reasons scientists study fossils.

A fossil can form when tree sap traps an animal. The sap hardens into amber. The animal is still inside.

Tell how amber might help scientists.

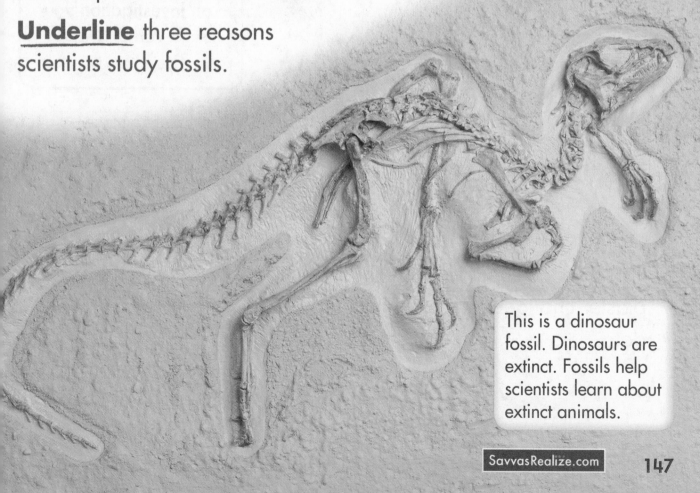

This is a dinosaur fossil. Dinosaurs are extinct. Fossils help scientists learn about extinct animals.

How can rocks crack?

Follow a Procedure

☑ **1.** Push the foil end of the sponge into the plaster. Keep the other end of the sponge out.

☑ **2.** Wait 1 day. Pull out the sponge. Do not pull out the foil. **Observe. Record.**

☑ **3.** Fill the foil with water. Put the cup in a freezer. Wait 1 day.

☑ **4.** Observe the cup. How has the plaster changed? Record your data.

Materials

plastic cup with plaster of paris

sponge with foil

water

safety goggles

latex-free gloves (optional)

Inquiry Skill

In an **investigation** you observe carefully and record your results.

Be careful! Wear safety goggles.

Wash your hands if you get plaster on them.

Do not eat plaster or get it in your eyes.

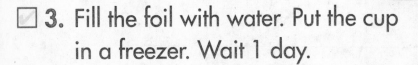

Observations

After 1 day	
After freezing	

Be careful! Wash your hands when you finish.

Analyze and Conclude

5. **Draw a Conclusion**   What caused the changes?

_____

6. **UNLOCK THE BIG ?** **Infer**   How are some cracks made in Earth's rocks?

_____

_____

_____

_____

Water on the Moon

Is there water on Earth's moon? NASA scientists sent a satellite to the moon to find out. They guided it to crash into a crater. Rock and other material shot up from the moon's surface. The scientists found signs of water in the material.

You need water. People working on the moon need water too.

This is an important discovery. It helps us understand the moon better. It may help future moon explorers too. People need water. But water is hard to carry into space. Finding water on the moon could solve the problem!

Write why water on the moon is an important discovery.

_____

_____

_____

Vocabulary Smart Cards

landform
glacier
weathering
erosion
fossil
extinct

Play a Game!

Cut out the cards.

Choose a card and give your partner clues.

Have your partner guess the word.

erosion

erosión

landform

accidente geográfico

fossil

fósil

glacier

glaciar

extinct

extinto

weathering

meteorización

a natural feature on Earth

formación natural en la Tierra

when wind, water, and other things move rock and soil

cuando el viento o el agua mueve rocas y suelo

large body of moving ice

gran masa de hielo que se mueve

a print or part of a plant or animal that lived long ago

huella o parte de una planta o animal que vivió hace mucho tiempo

when water, ice, or wind breaks down rocks

cuando el agua, el hielo o el viento rompe las rocas

a plant or animal that no longer lives on Earth

planta o animal que ya no existe en la Tierra

 152

Lesson 1

What are some kinds of land and water?

- Mountains and plains are landforms.
- Rivers and glaciers are kinds of water.

Lesson 2

What changes land?

- Earthquakes and volcanoes change land quickly.
- Weathering and erosion can change land slowly.

Lesson 3

What is a fossil?

- Fossils help scientists learn about how living things and Earth have changed over time.
- Extinct plants and animals no longer live on Earth.

Lesson 1

1. Vocabulary List three kinds of landforms.

_____

_____

_____

2. Contrast Write two ways a lake and an ocean are different.

_____

_____

_____

_____

3. Main Ideas and Details Read the paragraph below. **Underline** two details.

Glaciers are large bodies of moving ice.

Most of Earth's fresh water is found in glaciers.

Glaciers cause erosion as they move over land.

Lesson 2

4. Contrast Write how weathering and erosion are different. **Look** at this rock to help you explain.

_____

_____

5. Identify **Circle** the picture that shows erosion by water.

Lesson 3

6. **Describe** **Write** how a dead lizard becomes a fossil after the lizard is covered with mud and sand.

7. **Apply** You find fossils of fish and clams in the rocky walls of a canyon. **Write** what this tells you about this place in the past.

Got it?

☐ **Stop!** I need help with _____

▶ **Go!** Now I know _____

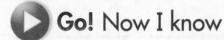

Does gravel, sand, or soil make the best imprint?

Materials

safety goggles

pencil

3 index cards

3 paper plates

plastic cup with gravel

plastic cup with soil

plastic cup with sand

shell

Sometimes sand slowly changes to rock. An imprint made by a plant or animal can become a fossil in the rock.

Ask a question.

Which will make the best imprint?

Make a prediction.

1. What makes the best imprint?
The best imprint will be made in

(a) gravel.

(b) sand.

(c) soil.

Plan a fair test.

Use the same amount of gravel, sand, and soil.

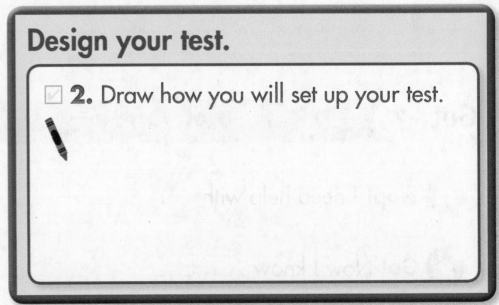

Design your test.

☑ **2.** Draw how you will set up your test.

Inquiry Skill
In a **fair test** you change only one thing.

☐ **3.** List your steps.

_____

_____

_____

Do your test.

☑ **4.** Follow your steps.

Collect and record data.

☑ **5.** Fill in the chart.

Be careful! Wash your hands when finished.

Tell your conclusion.

6. Does gravel, sand, or soil make the best imprint? Tell how you know.

_____

_____

_____

Earth's Materials

Science and Engineering Practices

1. Ask a question or define a problem.
2. Develop and use models.
3. Plan and carry out investigations.
4. Analyze and interpret data.
5. Use math and computational thinking.
6. Construct explanations or design solutions.
7. Engage in argument from evidence.
8. Obtain, evaluate, and communicate information.

Make a Poster

- Work with a partner.
- Make a poster that describes the different materials from which Earth is made.
- Write a title at the top of the poster.
- Cut out or draw pictures that show rocks, soil, and water.
- Write a caption for each picture.
- Tell your partner one way that these materials can change over time.

Erosion

- Gather samples of sand, soil, and clay. Place the samples in separate containers.
- Make model hills. Use books to raise one end of the containers.
- Pour the same amount of water over each sample. Observe what happens.
- Which sample had the most erosion? Which had the least?
- Based on your results, what kind of hill would have the most erosion by water? Explain.

Make a Puzzle

- Draw a map on heavy paper.
- Include different kinds of land and bodies of water.
- Label each kind of landform. Label each kind of body of water.
- Cut your map into pieces to make a puzzle.
- Give your puzzle to a partner to put together.
- Tell your partner about your map.

Model Earthquake Damage

- Use materials to make a model building on a tabletop. You might use sugar cubes, playing cards, or other materials.
- Bump the table lightly to model an earthquake.
- What happened to the building?
- How could you change your building to make it stay standing through an earthquake?

What does he want to ask?

The Nature of Science

Tell a partner what makes this boy a scientist.

What is science?

What are the mystery objects?

Scientists listen to sounds to learn new things.

Materials

6 mystery boxes

☐ **1. Observe** Shake each box. Listen to the sound.

Inquiry Skill You **infer** by making a good guess based on observations.

☐ **2.** Look at the pictures. What could make each sound?

☐ **3. Infer** Write the letter of the box by each picture.

rice   tissue   5 noodles   paper clip   toothpick   2 metal marbles

☐ **4.** Open each box to find out what is inside.

Explain Your Results

5. Communicate Think like a scientist. Explain how you decided what was in each box.

_____

_____

_____

_____

_____

Picture Clues

Pictures can give you **clues** about what you read.

Scientists

Scientists use tools to investigate. This girl is a scientist. She measures. She observes. She observes some more. Soon she will learn something new!

Practice It!

Look at the picture. What are two tools that scientists use?

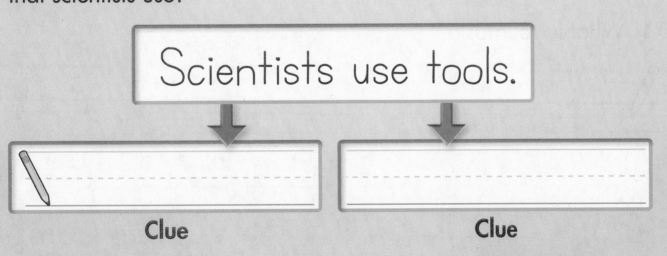

Scientists use tools.

Clue   Clue

Strike Up a Band!

Sounds can be loud or soft. Sounds can be high or low. All kinds of objects make sounds. The same object can make many different sounds. You will use materials to make sounds. You will design an instrument that can make loud, soft, high, and low sounds. You will test your instrument.

Find a Problem

☐ **1.** What is your task?

Test different instruments.

Find out how they make sounds.

Find out which ones make louder and softer sounds.

☐ **2.** Write about and draw what you discover.

Plan and Draw

☐ **3.** Draw an instrument here.

☐ **4.** How are rubber bands like parts of stringed instruments?

5. How are boxes like parts of drums or stringed instruments?

6. How are long tubes or containers like parts of different stringed or wood instruments?

Choose Materials

Look at the materials. Think about how to make an instrument that makes different sounds.

☐ **7.** What could make your design difficult?

☐ **8.** Pick one material you did not choose. Tell why you did not use that material.

☐ **9.** Draw what your instrument will look like. Label the parts.

Make and Test

Build your sound instrument.

☐ **10.** Draw your finished instrument below.

Tell how you make your instrument work.

11. How do you make a louder sound?	
12. How do you make a softer sound?	
13. How do you make a higher sound?	
14. How do you make a lower sound?	

Record and Share

☐ **15. Compare** your instrument with those of your classmates. How are they the same?

_____

_____

_____

_____

_____

_____

☐ **16.** How are the instruments different?

_____

_____

_____

_____

_____

☐ **17. Explain** how you would change your instrument. Draw.

What questions do scientists ask?

Envision It!

Tell one question scientists might ask about Mars.

my planeT DiaRY DISCOVERY

Read Together

Lunch is served! This astronaut put water back into her food. She is ready to eat!

Astronauts take food with them when they take off from the Kennedy Space Center in Florida. Scientists found a way to take food into space.

Many foods, like soup and macaroni and cheese, contain water. Scientists take water out of food so the food lasts longer. Astronauts put water back into the food before they eat it.

Tell what else scientists might need in space.

Word to Know

inquiry

Scientists

People who study the world around them are scientists. You are a scientist too. Scientists use inquiry to learn. **Inquiry** means asking questions and looking for answers.

This person asks questions about space. He uses a telescope to find answers.

This person is looking for answers to his questions about space.

⊙ **Picture Clues** How is the scientist learning about space? **Look** at the picture. **Write** what you see.

> The scientist is learning about space.

He is using a telescope.	
Clue	Clue

Scientists ask questions about plants.

Questions

Scientists ask questions about the world. Scientists ask questions about plants and animals. They ask questions about rocks and soil. They ask questions about space too. Scientists use inquiry to find answers to their questions.

Scientists know plants need soil to live and grow. They know there is no soil in space. They asked, "How might plants be grown in space without soil?" Then they looked for an answer.

Underline a question that scientists asked.

Write a question you might ask about plants in space.

Discovery

Scientists discovered ways to grow plants without soil. They found out what nutrients plants need from soil. Then they added the nutrients to water. They put the roots of some plants in the water. They observed how the plants grew. Scientists shared what they learned. They explained how plants could grow in space without soil. Now they can grow plants in space.

(Circle) the discovery that scientists made.

Lightning Lab

Questions, Please
Write three questions that a scientist might ask about plants.

Draw an X to show where nutrients were added.

Scientists found an answer to their question. They are growing plants without soil.

These tomatoes were grown without soil.

What kinds of skills do scientists use?

Envision It!

Tell what you could learn about this market by using your senses.

Inquiry **Explore It!**

How can you sort objects?

Think about the skills you use as you do this activity.

Materials

paper shapes

☐ **1. Observe** Work alone. Think of one way to classify the shapes. Sort into groups.

I classified the shapes by _____.

☐ **2.** Work with a group. Classify them in another way.

We classified the shapes by _____.

Explain Your Results

3. Communicate What skills did you use to sort the shapes?

_____

_____

_____

Word to Know

observe

Different Ways to Learn

Scientists learn about the world around them. They find out what they know in many different ways. Scientists use their senses.

Scientists do experiments to learn. They do experiments again and again to make sure they get the same results.

These scientists want to know how tall the plant will grow.

Scientists learn from each other too. They ask each other, "How do you know?" They share what they learn. They give answers. They tell how they know.

Why might scientists want to learn from each other?

Science Skills

Observe

Scientists observe to find out about the world. You **observe** when you use your senses to find out about something.

How do you know when an apple is ripe? You might look at the color. Some people tap it to hear how it sounds. You might feel it and smell it too. You will know if it is ripe when you taste it!

Predict

Scientists use what they observe to predict. You predict when you tell what you think will happen.

How might scientists predict how many apples will grow? They may think about how many apples grew the year before.

Picture Clues How do you know this apple tree is healthy?

_____

_____

_____

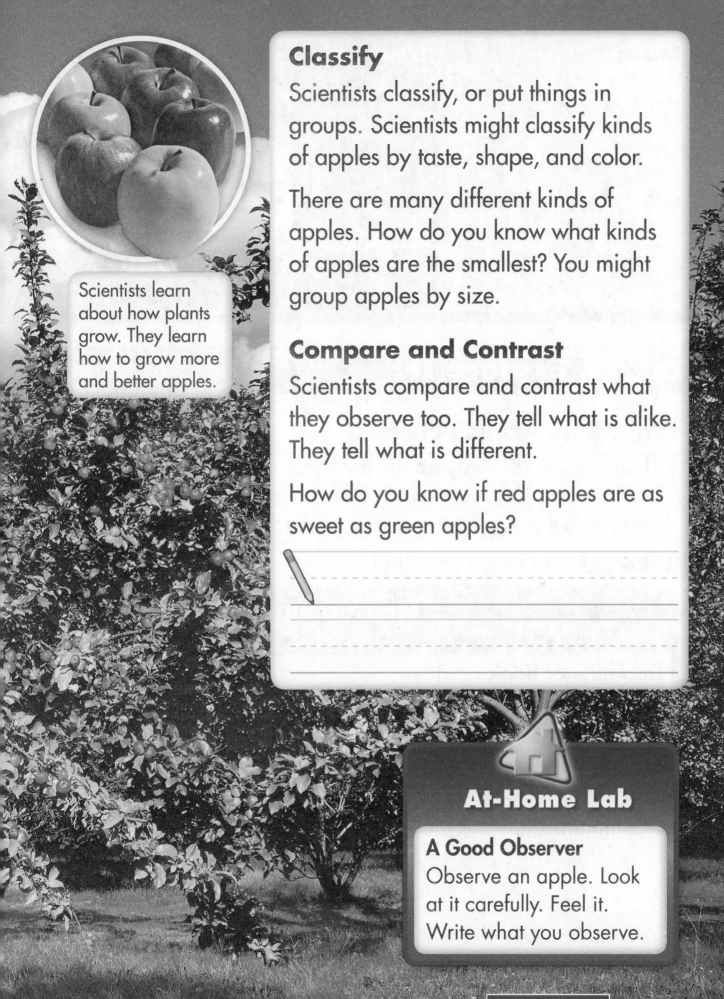

Classify

Scientists classify, or put things in groups. Scientists might classify kinds of apples by taste, shape, and color.

There are many different kinds of apples. How do you know what kinds of apples are the smallest? You might group apples by size.

Compare and Contrast

Scientists compare and contrast what they observe too. They tell what is alike. They tell what is different.

How do you know if red apples are as sweet as green apples?

_____

_____

_____

Scientists learn about how plants grow. They learn how to grow more and better apples.

At-Home Lab

A Good Observer
Observe an apple. Look at it carefully. Feel it. Write what you observe.

How do scientists use tools and stay safe?

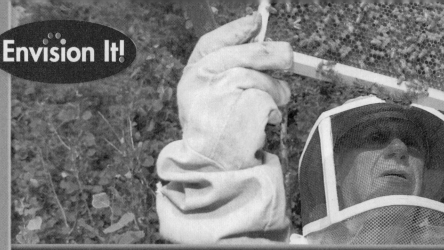

Envision It!

Tell one observation the beekeeper might make.

Inquiry

Explore It!

Which tool works better?

☐ 1. Use both tools. **Measure** the thickness of a book. Measure the height of a desk. Measure the length of your chalkboard.

☐ 2. **Record** your data in the chart.

Materials

meterstick

metric ruler

	Measurement (cm)	Which tool worked better?
Thickness of book		
Height of desk		
Length of chalkboard		

Explain Your Results

3. **Communicate** Did the same tool always work better? Explain.

_____

_____

_____

Word to Know

tool

Tools

Scientists use many different kinds of tools. A **tool** is something that is used to do work.

Some tools make objects look bigger. A hand lens helps a scientist observe a bee up close. Scientists use tools to stay safe too. A bee scientist wears a face cover and a body cover. The scientist wears gloves too.

You can use a hand lens to study insects.

Look at the picture of the bee. **Tell** what the bee's wings look like under the hand lens.

Use a hand lens to look at this picture. **Draw** what you see.

More Tools

You use many different kinds of tools to learn. Some tools are used to measure. Some tools help you stay safe. Read about the tools on these pages.

(Circle) two tools that are used to measure length.

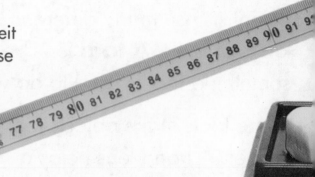

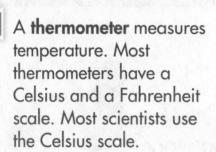

A **thermometer** measures temperature. Most thermometers have a Celsius and a Fahrenheit scale. Most scientists use the Celsius scale.

You can use a **meterstick** to measure how long something is. Scientists use a meterstick to measure in centimeters.

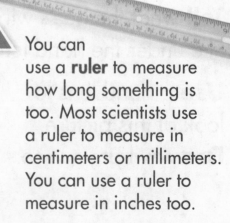

You can use a **ruler** to measure how long something is too. Most scientists use a ruler to measure in centimeters or millimeters. You can use a ruler to measure in inches too.

You can use **safety goggles** to protect your eyes.

You can use a **magnet** to see if an object is made of certain metals.

Draw an X on the tool you would use to measure time.

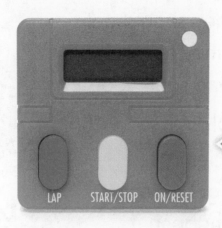

A **stopwatch** or **timer** measures how long something takes.

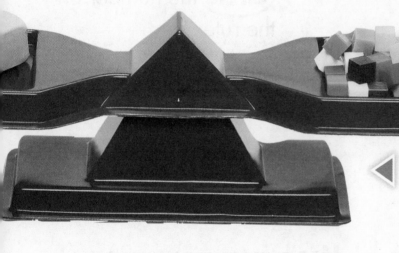

A **pan balance** is used to measure how much mass an object has. Objects that have a lot of mass feel heavy. Objects that do not have a lot of mass feel light.

You can use a **measuring cup** to measure volume. Volume is how much space something takes up.

Tell one way people might use a measuring cup at home.

Observe with Tools

Groups of scientists record the steps they take to answer questions. Another group of scientists may follow these steps. They should get the same answers if they follow the same steps and use the same tools.

Scientists compare what they observe with other scientists. Sometimes scientists get different answers. This might happen if a measuring tool is not used correctly. This might happen if the object being measured changes too. Scientists measure more than once to be sure their answers are correct.

Look at the picture. How long is the leaf? Circle the number on the ruler.

At-Home Lab

Measure Temperature
Use a thermometer to measure the outside temperature. Record the temperature in Fahrenheit and Celsius.

Use a measuring cup to measure two liquids.

OZ

Compare your measurements with a partner's measurements.

Safety Tips

Use these tips to stay safe when you observe.

- Listen to your teacher's instructions.
- Never taste or smell materials.
- Wear safety goggles when needed.
- Tie your hair back when needed.
- Handle tools carefully.
- Keep your workplace neat and clean.
- Clean up spills immediately.
- Wash your hands well after every activity.

(Circle) the tips that are hardest for you to remember.

Draw an X on two ways these people are staying safe.

Lesson 4

How do scientists find answers?

This scientist takes samples of the grass every year. **Tell** how the grass might change.

Inquiry Explore It!

What conclusion can you draw?

Materials

chips   plastic cup

☐ 1. Have a partner pick up the chips one at a time and put them in the cup.

☐ 2. Count the number of seconds that pass. **Record** how long it took to move all the chips.

Explain Your Results

3. **Draw a Conclusion** If you did this again, would you have the same result? Explain.

4. How could you improve your test?

UNLOCK
THE BIG
? I will know
why scientists repeat
investigations.

Words to Know

conclusion
hypothesis

Repeat Investigations

Scientists learn about the world around them. First they ask questions. Then they investigate. You investigate when you look for answers.

Scientists repeat investigations before they draw conclusions. A **conclusion** is what you decide after you think about all you know. You should be able to draw similar conclusions when you repeat an investigation.

For example, one scientist measures the height of the tallest tree in a forest. Others repeat the measurement. They get similar answers. They draw a conclusion.

Explain what would happen if other people repeat the same investigation as the scientist in the picture.

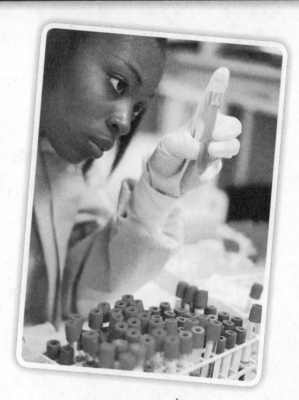

Scientists make conclusions from what they learn when they investigate.

Scientific Methods

Scientific methods are ways of finding answers. Some scientists use scientific methods when they do experiments. Scientific methods may have these steps. Sometimes scientists do the steps in a different order. Scientists do not always do all of the steps.

Ask a question.

Ask a question that you want answered.

Do seeds need water to grow?

Make your hypothesis.

A **hypothesis** is a possible answer to your question.

If seeds are watered, then they will grow because seeds need water.

Plan a fair test.

Change only one thing. Keep everything else the same. Record your steps. Someone else should get the same answer if they follow your steps.

Write the words water and no water to label the pots.

Use the same kinds of pots and soil. Water only one pot.

190

Do your test.

Test your hypothesis. Repeat your test. See if your results are the same.

Collect and record your data.

Keep records of what you observe. Use words, numbers, or drawings to help.

Go Green

Repeat a Test
Do plants need sunlight? Think of a hypothesis. Plan a test. Test your hypothesis. Record your steps. Repeat your test.

Tell your conclusion.

Think about the results of your test. Decide if your hypothesis is supported or not supported. Tell what you decide.

Seeds need water to grow.

Circle the question. **Underline** the hypothesis.

Explain what you think would happen if someone else followed the same steps in this investigation.

_____

_____

_____

How do scientists collect and share data?

Envision It!

Write what you observe about the rocks.

What are different ways you can collect and share data?

How many boys and girls are in your class?

 1. Use the Tally Chart.

Make 1 mark for each boy.

Make 1 mark for each girl.

Tally Chart	
Boys	
Girls	

 2. Use the Picture Chart.

Color 1 picture for each boy.

Color 1 picture for each girl.

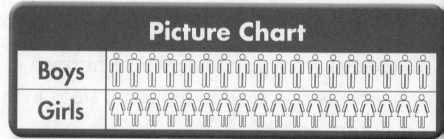

Picture Chart	
Boys	
Girls	

Explain Your Results

3. Communicate Share your charts with your family.
Which did they like better? Explain.

_____

Word to Know

data

Collect Data

Scientists collect data to learn new things. **Data** is what you observe. You use your senses to collect data.

Scientists make conclusions from the data and from what they already know. Scientists infer when they make conclusions. You infer when you use what you know to explain something.

Underline what you use to observe data.

○ Picture Clues **Look** at the picture. What can you infer about the rocks?

Record Data

Scientists record what they observe and measure. They look at the data carefully.

Scientists can learn new things when they record data. Sometimes they find patterns. Sometimes they learn what is the same. Sometimes they learn what is different.

Look at the three rocks. **Measure** how wide each rock is with a ruler. **Write** the data in centimeters.

granite

basalt

pumice

At-Home Lab

Observe and Compare
Find three leaves in your neighborhood. Look at them carefully. Compare the shapes and colors. Measure them in inches.

Show Data

Scientists use charts and graphs to show data. A chart helps you organize data. A bar graph helps you compare data.

Use your data. **Fill in** this empty chart.

Comparing Rocks	
	Width (centimeters)
Granite	
Basalt	
Pumice	

Use this empty bar graph. **Fill in** the bar for each rock.

Comparing Rocks

Width of Rock (centimeters)

9
8
7
6
5
4
3
2
1
0

Granite   Basalt   Pumice

Make a conclusion from your data.
Which rock is the widest?

_____

- -

What skills do scientists use?

Follow a Procedure

☐ **1.** Stir 1 spoonful of salt into the salt cup.

Materials

2 plastic cups with water

spoon

2 ice cubes

salt

timer

Inquiry Skill
You **interpret data** when you decide what the data means.

plain

salt

☐ **2.** Put 1 ice cube in each cup. Start the timer.

☐ **3.** Check the timer when the first ice cube melts. **Record.**

☐ **4.** Stop the timer when the second ice cube melts. Record.

Ice Cube Data		
	Time to Melt (minutes)	
Plain water		
Salt water		

Analyze and Conclude

5. **Interpret Data**   Did the ice cubes melt at the same rate?
   Explain.

_____

_____

_____

_____

6. UNLOCK THE BIG ?   Name three science skills you used.

_____

_____

_____

_____

Shonte Wright

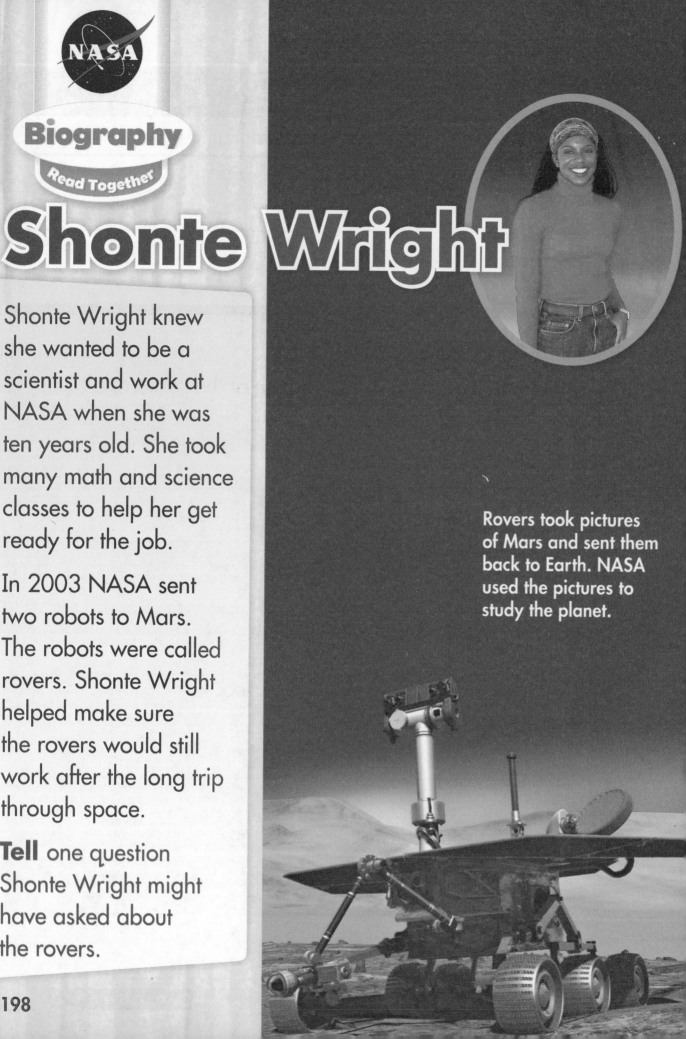

Shonte Wright knew she wanted to be a scientist and work at NASA when she was ten years old. She took many math and science classes to help her get ready for the job.

In 2003 NASA sent two robots to Mars. The robots were called rovers. Shonte Wright helped make sure the rovers would still work after the long trip through space.

Tell one question Shonte Wright might have asked about the rovers.

Rovers took pictures of Mars and sent them back to Earth. NASA used the pictures to study the planet.

Vocabulary Smart Cards

inquiry
observe
tool
conclusion
hypothesis
data

Play a Game!

Cut out the cards.

Work with a partner.

One person puts the cards picture side up.

The other person puts the cards picture side down.

Work together to match each word with its meaning.

conclusion

conclusión

inquiry

indagación

hypothesis

hipótesis

observe

observar

data

datos

tool

instrumento

asking questions and
looking for answers

hacer preguntas y
buscar respuestas

what you decide after
you think about all
you know

lo que decides
después de pensar
en lo que sabes

to use your senses
to find out about
something

usar tus sentidos para
descubrir algo

a possible answer to
a question

respuesta posible a
una pregunta

something that is
used to do work

algo que se usa para
hacer trabajo

what you observe

lo que observas

Lesson 1

What questions do scientists ask?

- Scientists use inquiry to learn about things.
- Scientists discover ways to solve problems.

Lesson 2

What kinds of skills do scientists use?

- Scientists observe and predict.
- Scientists classify and compare.

Lesson 3

How do scientists use tools and stay safe?

- Scientists use many different tools to learn.
- Hand lenses, rulers, and gloves are tools.

Lesson 4

How do scientists find answers?

- Scientists investigate and draw conclusions.
- A hypothesis is a possible answer to a question.

Lesson 5

How do scientists collect and share data?

- Scientists use their senses to collect data.
- Scientists show data in charts and bar graphs.

Lesson 1

1. **Picture Clues** The girl in the picture is using inquiry to learn about plants. What is she learning about the plant?

_____

_____

2. **Apply** Some scientists ask questions about space. **Write** a question you have about space.

_____

_____

_____

_____

Lesson 2

3. **Vocabulary** **Complete** the sentence.

You _____ when you use your senses to find out about something.

4. **Describe** **Look** at the picture. **Write** something you observe about this rock.

_____

_____

_____

_____

Lesson 3

5. **Classify** What is a tool that can help you stay safe?
   Fill in the bubble.

   Ⓐ meterstick   Ⓒ goggles

   Ⓑ stopwatch   Ⓓ magnet

Lesson 4

6. **Evaluate** Why might a scientist repeat investigations?

   _____

   _____

Lesson 5

7. **Analyze Look** at the picture.
   What can you infer about this plant?

   _____

   _____

Got it?

☐ **Stop!** I need help with _____

   _____

▶ **Go!** Now I know _____

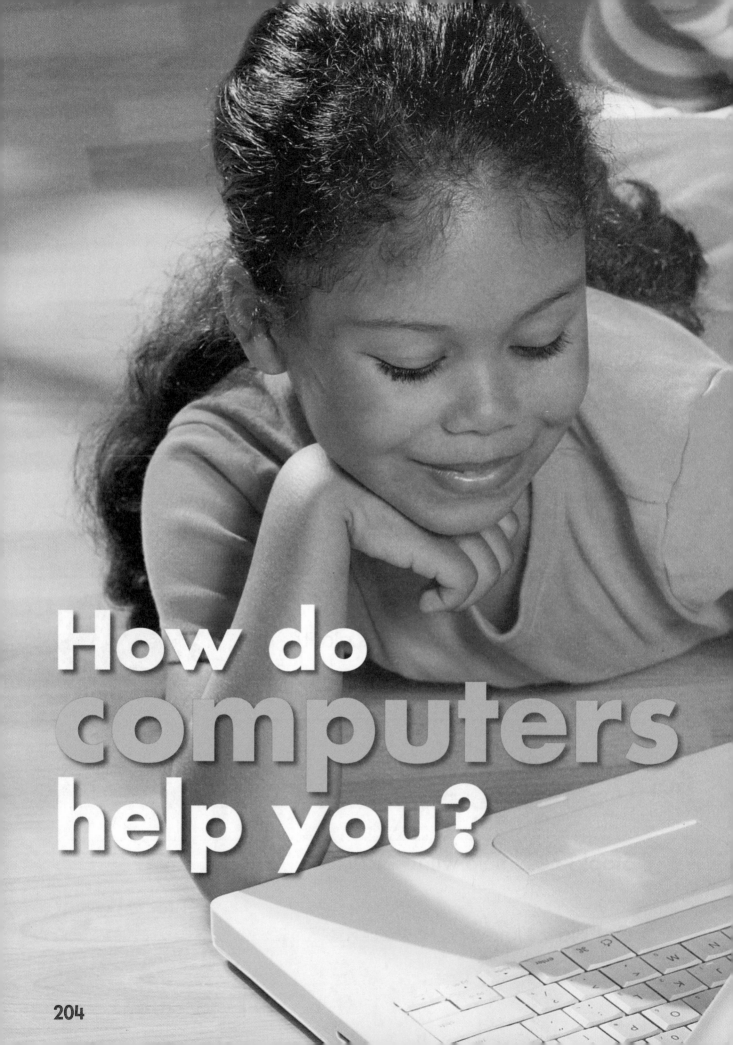

How do computers help you?

Technology and Tools

Try It! How can you keep an ice cube from melting?

STEM Activity All Bound Up!

Lesson 1 What is technology?

Lesson 2 How do people design new things?

Lesson 3 How do we use tools and machines?

Investigate It! How can a machine ring a bell?

Science, Engineering, and Technology

Design It! How would you design a pencil?

Tell how you use a computer.
Tell about another kind of technology that is important to you.

 How do people solve problems?

How can you keep an ice cube from melting?

☐ **1.** Put an ice cube in each of 2 cups.

☐ **2.** **Design** a way to keep an ice cube from melting. Make and test your design.

☐ **3.** Wait 10 minutes. **Observe.** Compare the 2 ice cubes.

Explain Your Results

4. **Communicate**
Draw and label your **design.**

Materials

2 ice cubes

2 plastic cups

wax paper

newspaper

aluminum foil

cotton balls

foam packing peanuts

masking tape

Inquiry Skill
You **communicate** when you draw and label diagrams.

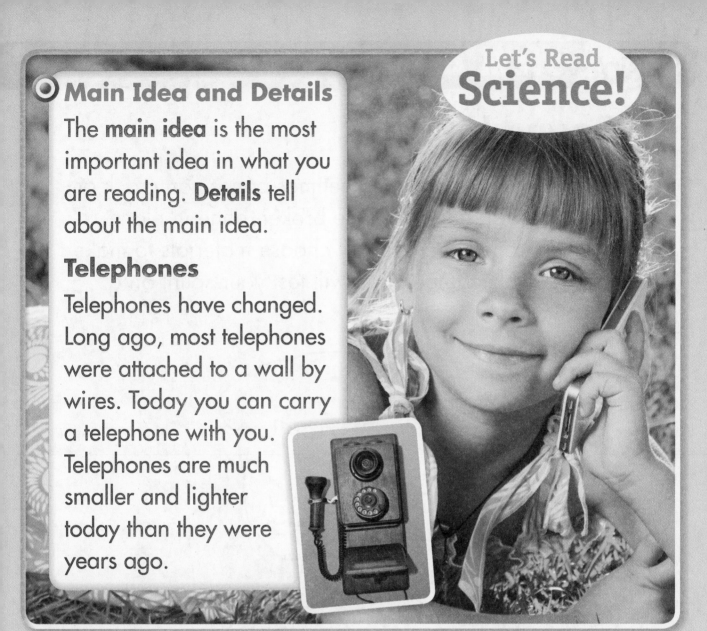

Main Idea and Details

The **main idea** is the most important idea in what you are reading. **Details** tell about the main idea.

Telephones

Telephones have changed. Long ago, most telephones were attached to a wall by wires. Today you can carry a telephone with you. Telephones are much smaller and lighter today than they were years ago.

Let's Read Science!

Practice It!

Write two details about how telephones have changed.

Telephones have changed over the years.

Main Idea

Detail

Detail

All Bound Up!

Your body has many bones. Sometimes bones can crack or break. A splint or a cast holds the broken bone in place. This helps the bone heal. You will choose materials to make a splint for a broken finger. You will test your splint on a model finger.

Learn how splints and casts help bones heal. Think about how splints and casts are the same and different.

Find a Problem

☐ **1.** What will happen if a cast or splint cannot protect a bone?

_____

_____

_____

_____

_____

_____

☐ **2.** Why do casts and splints have to be different shapes and sizes?

_____

_____

_____

_____

_____

_____

Plan and Draw

☐ **3.** Trace your finger.

☐ **4.** What size and shape should your splint be? Why?

☐ **5.** Should your splint be loose or tight? Why?

☐ **6.** Draw a picture of what your splint will look like.

Choose Materials

Look at the materials. Think about how to make a splint.

☐ **7.** List the materials you will use for your splint. What could make your design difficult?

☐ **8.** Pick one material you did not choose. Write why you will not use that material.

☐ **9.** Draw how you will use the materials you chose to make your splint.

Make and Test

Make your splint. Use a piece of celery as a model finger.

☐ **10.** Draw your finished splint. **Compare** it to your drawing from Step 9. Did you follow your plan? **Explain.**

☐**11.** How can you test the splint? Try it. Write the steps you followed.

_____
_____
_____
_____
_____
_____

☐**12.** What happened when you tested your splint?

_____
_____
_____
_____
_____
_____

Record and Share

Compare your splint with a splint made by another group.

☐ **13.** How are the splints alike?

_____

_____

_____

_____

_____

☐ **14.** How are the splints different?

_____

_____

_____

_____

_____

□**15.** Tell how you could redesign your splint. Draw the new splint.

Envision It!

Tell what problem the train helps solve.

my planet Diary

INVENTION!

Read Together

Engineers have designed a train that uses magnets instead of engines. These trains are called Maglev trains. They are faster and quieter than trains that use engines. Maglev trains float about one to ten centimeters above a guideway. The magnets on the bottoms of the trains and the magnets on the guideway help move the train along. Maglev trains can travel faster than 300 miles per hour!

Use a ruler. **Draw** a line that is ten centimeters tall to show how high Maglev trains can float.

guideway

Words to Know

technology

invent

Technology

People ride in cars. People use computers. We can do these things because of technology. **Technology** is the use of science to solve problems.

Sometimes people use technology to invent things. **Invent** means to make something for the first time.

Technology has made many things easier for people. Cars and trains are technology. They help people travel long distances. However, technology does not solve every problem. Cars and trains can break and stop working.

Tell one way computers help people. **Tell** one problem computers do not solve.

Scientists make cars that use electricity. These cars help reduce pollution.

SavvasRealize.com

219

Solve Problems

Engineers are people who design new things. They look for better ways to solve problems. They use science and technology to invent and discover new things.

Some people have trouble seeing. People used technology to solve this problem. People invented glasses. Glasses help people see better. Glasses are technology.

◉ **Main Idea and Details** **Underline** a problem that technology solves.

Read about technology below. **Pick** one technology. **Tell** what kind of problem it solves.

Technology Over Time

1879
The light bulb is mass-produced.

1885
A car that uses gasoline is invented.

1903
The Wright brothers fly their plane in Kitty Hawk, North Carolina.

1946
The first microwave oven is built.

Help People

Technology can help people stay healthy too. Doctors use technology to find out why people are sick.

People invented X rays. X rays are tools doctors can use to see inside people. Doctors can help people to get well after they find out what is wrong.

Draw another kind of technology. **Tell** what problem it solves. **Tell** one problem it does not solve.

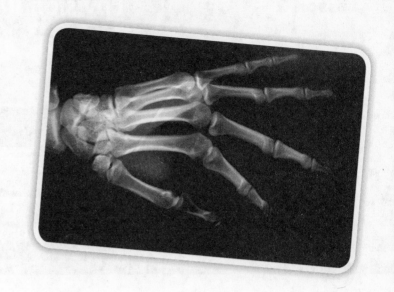

1975
The digital camera is invented.

2008
Text messaging is popular.

Draw something you would like to invent.

How do people design new things?

Envision It!

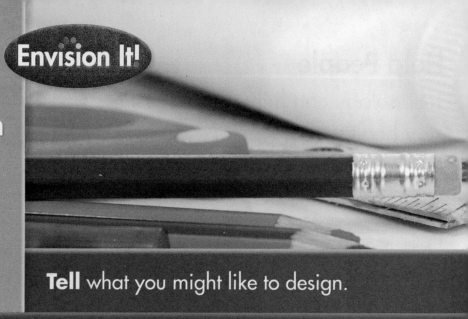

Tell what you might like to design.

Inquiry **Explore It!**

How can you keep warm water warm?

☑ **1.** Fill 2 cups with warm water. **Measure** both temperatures. **Record.**

☑ **2.** **Cover** one with foil, plastic, or a paper towel.

☑ **3.** Wait 10 minutes. Measure. Record.

Materials

warm water

plastic wrap

tape

paper towel

foil

2 cups   thermometer

Temperature Chart

Cup of Water	Starting (°C)	After 10 min (°C)
Not covered		
Covered		

Explain Your Results

4. Infer How did you keep the water warm?

_____

Words to Know

goal
material

A Problem and a Goal

Engineers think about a problem that needs to be solved. Then they set a goal to find a solution to the problem. A **goal** is something you want to do.

Chester Greenwood lived a long time ago in Maine. Chester had a problem. His ears got very cold in the winter. He set a goal. He wanted to find a way to keep his ears warm.

Think about a problem you want to solve. **Write** your goal.

Maine can get very cold in the winter.

Plan and Draw

Engineers plan and draw before they make new things. Sometimes they plan and draw more than once.

Chester Greenwood planned to use a heavy wool scarf to stay warm. He tied it around his head. It kept his ears warm. However, the wool scarf was very itchy.

Chester wanted to find a better solution to his problem. Chester planned again. He planned to make earflaps to cover his ears.

Look at the drawings to see what Chester's plan might have looked like.

1. Make wire loops.

2. Cover loops.

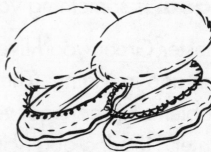

3. Sew covers around wire loops.

Think of a problem. **Draw** something that would solve the problem. **Tell** how it solves your problem.

Choose Materials

Engineers choose materials to make new things. A **material** is what something is made of. Materials can be very different. Some materials are soft. Other materials are hard. Some materials are light. Other materials are heavy.

(Circle) materials you would want to use to keep your ears warm. **Tell** why.

At-Home Lab

Different Designs
Find out about two kinds of shoes. What are the shoes used for? Tell how the designs are different.

cotton

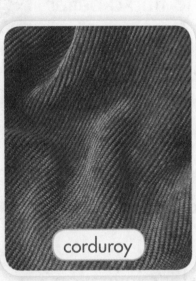

corduroy

Draw a different material you might want to use. **Tell** about your drawing.

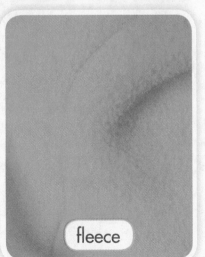

fleece

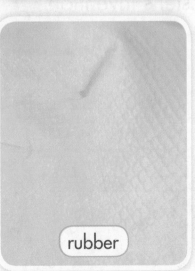

rubber

Make and Test

Engineers make and test the solution to their problem. They want to find out how well their design works. Sometimes they change their design. They do this to make their design better.

Chester made oval loops out of wire. Then he covered the loops with soft materials. Chester's earflaps kept his ears warm.

However, Chester wanted to find a better way to keep the earflaps in place. He changed his design. He made his design better by adding a flat steel spring to fit over his head. This kept the earflaps in place over his ears.

Underline why Chester changed his design.

How could you make Chester's invention even better?

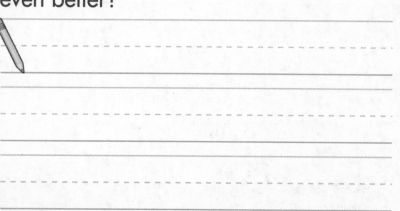

Record and Share

Engineers record what they have done. They write about their designs. They draw and label their designs too. Recording helps them remember what they have done. Sometimes engineers share what they have done with others.

Write headband or earflap to label the parts of these earmuffs.

This girl is wearing earmuffs. There are many different kinds of earmuffs today.

How do we use tools and machines?

Envision It!

Tell what kinds of tools you think were used to build this tree house.

Inquiry **Explore It!**

How does a lever work?

A lever is a type of simple machine.

☐ **1.** Make a lever. Set up the ruler, pencil, and book as shown.

☐ **2.** Push down on the end of the lever. **Observe.**

☐ **3.** Repeat with the pencil at 15 cm and at 10 cm.

Explain Your Results

4. Communicate When was it easiest to lift the book?

Materials

wooden ruler

book

unsharpened pencil

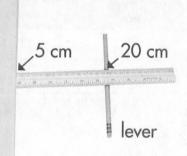

5 cm   20 cm

lever

UNLOCK THE BIG ?

I will know about tools and simple machines. I will know how some body parts can be used as tools.

Words to Know

simple machine

Tools and Machines

Suppose you want to move an object. You might use a tool to help you. A machine is a tool that can make work easier. Sometimes tools and machines can do things that your body cannot do on its own.

A **simple machine** is a tool with few or no moving parts. A screw is a simple machine. A screw is used to hold things together.

Draw one object that is held together by screws.

A wagon is a machine. You can use a wagon to move heavy things. You can use a wagon to move many things at one time.

Simple Machines

There are many different kinds of tools and machines. Levers and wedges are simple machines. Pulleys and inclined planes are simple machines too.

Pulleys move an object up, down, or sideways. An inclined plane is flat. It is higher at one end than at the other. An inclined plane makes it easier to move things.

Look at the picture below. **Circle** the part that is the inclined plane.

pulley

Tell how the pulley moves the flag.

Suppose you need to move a heavy box. What could you use to help you move it? **Design** a tool to help you.

Body Parts as Tools

Think about different parts of your body. You can use some parts of your body as tools. You can use your body to do work.

shovel

A lever is a tool. A lever can be used to move things. A shovel is a lever. It can move dirt. You can use your arms as levers. You can use your arms to pick things up.

arms

tongs

These tongs are made of two levers. Levers can be used to grasp objects. You can use your hands as levers. You can use your hands to grasp a ball.

hands

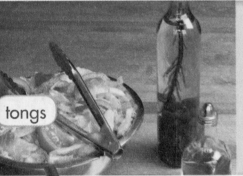

knife

A wedge is a tool. A wedge is used to push things apart. A knife is a wedge. You can use your teeth as a wedge. You can use your teeth to cut and chew food.

teeth

Underline two simple machines on this page.

What other body part can you use as a tool? **Explain.**

_____

_____

_____

Tools in Nature
Make a model of an animal body part. Tell how it is like a tool. Tell how it is different from a tool.

Animal Body Parts as Tools

Think about different animals. Animals use body parts as tools. Gophers use their claws to dig into the ground. Woodpeckers use their beaks to drill into trees. Animals use their body parts to do work.

Tell what body parts a dog might use as a tool.

The beaver has long front teeth. It uses its teeth as a wedge to cut into wood.

teeth

wedge

The blue jay uses its beak to hold on to food. Its beak is like two levers.

levers

beak

Draw another animal that can use body parts as tools.
Tell about the animal you drew.

The sea turtle uses its flippers as shovels, or levers. It kicks sand out of the way to build a nest.

lever

flippers

Badger claws are like wedges. The claws help the badger dig into the ground.

wedge

claws

How can a machine ring a bell?

Follow a Procedure

☐ 1. **Design** a way to ring a bell from one meter away. Use two simple machines.

☐ 2. Draw your plan.

Materials

bell   marble

common objects

meterstick

Inquiry Skill
You **infer** when you get ideas from what you learn.

234

3. Record what materials you will use.

4. Test your design.
My machine (**did / did not**) ring the bell.

5. Evaluate your design. How could you **redesign** your machine to ring the bell better?

Analyze and Conclude

6. **Communicate**   What simple machines did you use?

7. **Infer**   Think how you used a simple machine to solve a problem. How do simple machines help people solve problems?

Microchips

Microchips are everywhere! They are in e-book readers and microwaves. They are in computers too. Microchips are usually less than 1 centimeter on each side. A pea is less than 1 centimeter on each side too.

Engineers use microchips to develop new technology. Microchips let engineers make smaller computers. Microchips help computers give and take directions. For example, many runners use a small computer that has a microchip. The microchip shows how long it took the runner to run the race.

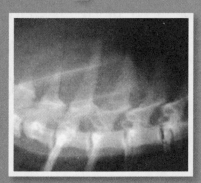

Microchips can help track lost dogs and cats. These chips are about the size of a grain of rice.

What new technology do you think engineers will develop soon?

Vocabulary Smart Cards

- technology
- invent
- goal
- material
- simple machine

Play a Game!

Cut out the cards.

Work with a group.

Tape a card to the back of each group member.

Give each person clues about his or her word.

Have everyone guess his or her word.

material

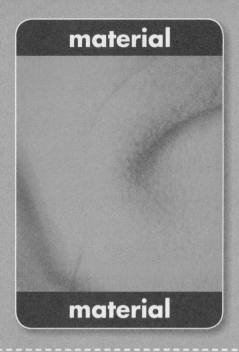

material

technology

tecnología

simple machine

máquina simple

invent

inventar

goal

objetivo

the use of science to solve problems

el uso de la ciencia para resolver problemas

what something is made of

de lo que está hecho algo

to make something for the first time

hacer algo por primera vez

tool with few or no moving parts

instrumento sin, o con pocas, partes que se mueven

something you want to do

algo que quieres hacer

Lesson 1 What is technology?

- Technology is the use of science to solve problems.
- Invent means to make something for the first time.

Lesson 2 How do people design new things?

- People set a goal, plan, draw, choose materials, make, test, record, and share.

Lesson 3 How do we use tools and machines?

- Simple machines can make work easier.
- You can use some parts of your body as tools.

Lesson 1

1. **Describe Think** about one kind of technology you use. **Write** how it helps you.

2. **Main Idea and Details Read** the paragraph below. **Underline** two details.

   Technology has changed the way people have fun. People listen to music on MP3 players. People use computers to play games.

Lesson 2

3. **Vocabulary Complete** the sentence. **Fill in** the bubble.
   Chester Greenwood wanted to find a way to keep his ears warm. He set a _____.

   Ⓐ problem   Ⓒ goal
   Ⓑ record   Ⓓ test

4. **Evaluate** Circle the earmuffs that you would want to wear. **Tell** why.

Lesson 3

5. **Classify Draw** a line from the picture to the term that goes with it.

(pulley)   (screw)   (inclined plane)

6. **Describe Write** one way you can use your hands as tools.

_____

_____

Got it?

⬜ **Stop!** I need help with _____

_____

▶ **Go!** Now I know _____

_____

How would you design a pencil?

The earliest versions of pencils were made by adults.
They made the pencils for adults to use. **Design** a pencil.

Find a problem.

☑ **1.** List three things you would change about a pencil.
Tell why you would make each change.

Change A:

Change B:

Change C:

Plan and draw.

2. Pick one thing to change. Make a step-by-step plan.
You will use the materials from the next page.
Tell how you would test your **design.**

3. Draw your design. Label each material.

Choose materials.

☐ **4.** Circle the materials you will use.

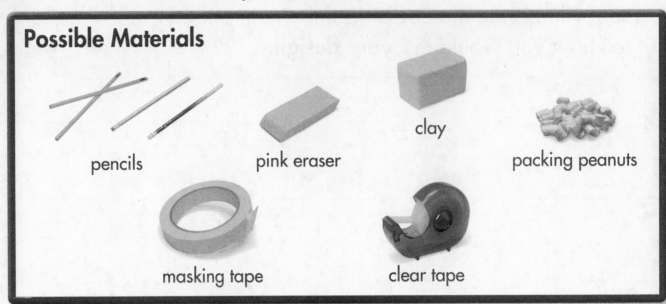

Possible Materials

pencils

pink eraser

clay

packing peanuts

masking tape

clear tape

☐ **5.** Tell how you will use each material.

Make and test.

6. Make the new pencil you **designed.** Follow your plan.

7. Test your pencil design by filling in the chart below.
   Use a regular pencil. Then use the pencil you designed.

Pencil Chart		
	Regular Pencil	**Pencil You Designed**
Print Pencil. **Pencil**		
Handwrite Pencil. *Pencil*		
Print 3 + 5 = 8. $3 + 5 = 8$		
Draw the hammer. 		

Record and share.

☑ **8.** Use your new pencil for one day.
Record when you used your pencil.
Record your **observations** about how well it worked.

9. What about your pencil **design** worked well?

_____
_____
_____

10. What about your pencil design did not work well?

_____
_____
_____

11. How could you **redesign** your pencil?

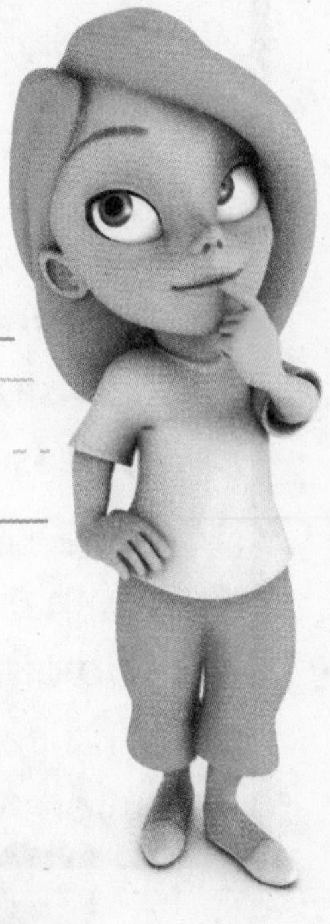

_____
_____
_____
_____

Performance-Based Assessment

Bus	Car	Walk

Science and Engineering Practices

1. Ask a question or define a problem.
2. Develop and use models.
3. Plan and carry out investigations.
4. Analyze and interpret data.
5. Use math and computational thinking.
6. Construct explanations or design solutions.
7. Engage in argument from evidence.
8. Obtain, evaluate, and communicate information.

Travel to School

- Do more classmates come to school on a bus, in a car, or by walking?
- Make a hypothesis.
- Use a chart and collect data.
- Tell your conclusion.

Design a Solution

- Think of a problem you want to solve.
- Plan and draw your solution in a notebook.
- Label your drawing.
- List the materials you would use.
- Share your design with a partner.

Write a Song

- Write a song about technology.
- Give your song a name and sing it to the class.

Metric and Customary Measurements

Science uses the metric system to measure things.
Metric measurement is used around the world.
Here is how different metric measurements
compare to customary measurements.

1 liter

1 cup

Fahrenheit

Celsius

Temperature
Water freezes at 0°C, or 32°F.
Water boils at 100°C, or 212°F.

Volume
One liter is greater
than 4 cups.

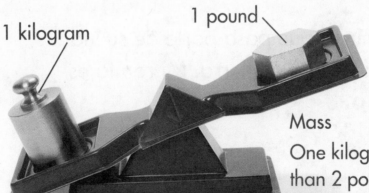

1 pound

1 kilogram

Mass
One kilogram is greater
than 2 pounds.

1 meter

1 foot

Length and Distance
One meter is longer than 3 feet.

Glossary

The glossary uses letters and signs to show how words are pronounced. The mark ′ is placed after a syllable with a primary or heavy accent. The mark ′ is placed after a syllable with a secondary or lighter accent.

To hear these vocabulary words and definitions, you can log on to the digital path's Vocabulary Smart Cards.

A

amphibian (am fib′ ē ən) An animal that lives part of its life in water and part of its life on land. My pet frog is an **amphibian.**

anfibio Animal que pasa parte de su vida en el agua y parte en tierra. Mi ranita es un **anfibio.**

camouflage (kam′ ə fläzh) A color or shape that makes an animal hard to see. Some animals use **camouflage** to hide themselves.

camuflaje Color o forma que hace que un animal sea difícil de ver. Algunos animales usan **camuflaje** para esconderse.

combine (kəm bīn′) To put two or more things together. I **combine** materials to make a kite.

combinar Unir dos o más cosas. Yo **combino** materiales para hacer una cometa.

conclusion (kən klü′ zhən) What you decide after you think about all you know. Scientists repeat their tests before drawing a **conclusion.**

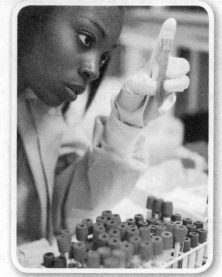

conclusión Lo que decides después de pensar en lo que sabes. Los científicos repiten sus pruebas antes de sacar una **conclusión.**

D

data (dā′ tə) What you observe. Scientists collect **data** while working.

datos Lo que observas. Los científicos reúnen **datos** cuando trabajan.

erosion (i rō′ zhən) When wind or water moves rocks and soil. **Erosion** washed away the sand near the ocean.

erosión Cuando el viento o el agua mueve rocas y suelo. La **erosión** arrastró la arena cerca del mar.

evaporate (i vap′ ə rāt) To change from a liquid to a gas. Water **evaporates** when it changes into water vapor.

evaporarse Cambiar de líquido a gas. El agua se **evapora** cuando se convierte en vapor de agua.

extinct (ek stingkt′) A plant or animal that no longer lives on Earth. Dinosaurs are **extinct.**

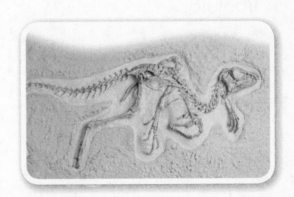

extinto Planta o animal que ya no existe en la Tierra. Los dinosaurios están **extintos.**

food chain (füd chān) A model that shows how energy passes from one living thing to another. Plants are part of **food chains.**

cadena alimentaria Modelo que muestra cómo se transmite la energía de un ser vivo a otro. Las plantas forman parte de **cadenas alimentarias.**

fossil (fos′ əl) A print or part of a plant or animal that lived long ago. The scientist found a dragonfly **fossil.**

fósil Huella o parte de una planta o animal que vivió hace mucho tiempo. El científico encontró el **fósil** de una libélula.

gas (gas) Matter that does not have its own size or shape. Bubbles are filled with **gas.**

gas Materia que no tiene tamaño ni forma propios. Las burbujas están llenas de **gas.**

glacier (glā′ shər) A large body of moving ice. **Glaciers** can be found in the Arctic.

glaciar Gran masa de hielo que se mueve. En el Ártico hay **glaciares.**

goal (gōl) Something you want to do. People set a **goal** to find a solution.

objetivo Algo que quieres hacer. Escogemos un **objetivo** para encontrar una solución.

habitat (hab′ ə tat) A place where a plant or animal lives. An arctic fox lives in a cold **habitat.**

hábitat Un lugar donde vive una planta o un animal. Un zorro ártico vive en un **hábitat** frío.

hypothesis (hī poth′ ə sis) A possible answer to a question. Scientists decide if a **hypothesis** is supported or not supported.

hipótesis Respuesta posible a una pregunta. Los científicos deciden si una **hipótesis** tiene bases firmes o no.

inquiry (in kwī′ rē) Asking questions and looking for answers. Scientists use **inquiry** to learn.

indagación Hacer preguntas y buscar respuestas. Los científicos hacen **indagaciones** para aprender.

invent (in vent′) To make something for the first time. Scientists **invented** cars that use both gasoline and electricity.

inventar Hacer algo por primera vez. Los científicos **inventaron** carros que usan tanto gasolina como electricidad.

landform (land′ fôrm) A natural feature on Earth. A plain is one kind of **landform.**

accidente geográfico Formación natural en la Tierra. Una llanura es un tipo de **accidente geográfico.**

liquid (lik′ wid) Matter that has its own volume but takes the shape of its container. The **liquid** changes shape in the tubes.

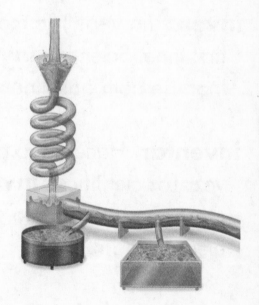

líquido Materia que tiene su propio volumen pero que toma la forma del recipiente que la contiene. El **líquido** cambia de forma dentro de los tubos.

material (mə tir′ ē əl) What something is made of. Fleece is a soft **material.**

material De lo que está hecho algo. El tejido polar es un **material** suave.

matter (mat′ ər) Anything that takes up space and has mass. Everything is made of **matter.**

materia Todo lo que ocupa espacio y tiene masa. Todo está hecho de **materia.**

mixture (miks′ chər) Something made up of two or more kinds of matter. This fruit salad is a **mixture** of different fruits.

mezcla Algo formado por varios tipos de materia. Esta ensalada es una **mezcla** de frutas.

nutrient (nü′ trē ənt) A material that living things need to live and grow. Many plants get **nutrients** from soil and water.

nutriente Un material que los seres vivos necesitan para vivir y crecer. Muchas plantas obtienen **nutrientes** del suelo y del agua.

observe (əb sėrv′) To use your senses to find out about something. You can **observe** how an apple looks, sounds, feels, smells, and tastes.

observar Usar tus sentidos para descubrir algo. Puedes **observar** el aspecto de una manzana, cómo suena, cómo es cuando la tocas, a qué huele y a qué sabe.

physical change (fiz′ ə kəl chānj) A change to matter without making it a new kind of matter. Sharpening a pencil causes a **physical change.**

cambio físico Un cambio a la materia que no la convierte en una materia nueva. Afilar la punta de un lápiz causa un **cambio físico.**

predator (pred′ ə tər) An animal that catches and eats another animal. A hawk is a fierce **predator.**

predador Animal que caza y se alimenta de otro animal. El halcón es un **predador** feroz.

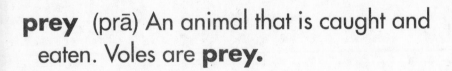

prey (prā) An animal that is caught and eaten. Voles are **prey.**

presa Animal que es cazado y comido. Las ratas de campo sirven de **presa.**

property (prop′ ər tē) Something about an object that you can observe with your senses. An object's color is one kind of **property.**

propiedad Algo en un objeto que puedes observar con tus sentidos. El color de un objeto es una **propiedad** de ese objeto.

R

roots (rütz) Parts of the plant that hold the plant in place and take in water and nutrients. **Roots** grow into the soil.

raíces Partes de la planta que la matienen en su lugar y que absorben agua y nutrientes.
Las **raíces** al crecer se entierran en el suelo.

S

simple machine (sim′ pəl mə shēn′) Tool with few or no moving parts. A **simple machine** can make work easier.

máquina simple Instrumento sin, o con pocas, partes que se mueven. Una **máquina simple** puede hacer que el trabajo sea más fácil.

solid (sol′ id) Matter that keeps its own size and shape. The case that holds the supplies is a **solid.**

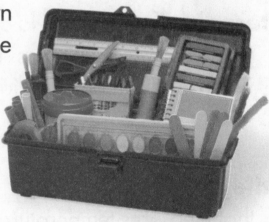

sólido Materia que mantiene tamaño y forma propios. La caja de útiles de pintura es un **sólido.**

stem (stem) Part of the plant that carries water and nutrients to the leaves. Some plants have a straight **stem.**

tallo Parte de la planta que lleva el agua y los nutrientes a las hojas. Algunas plantas tienen el **tallo** derecho.

T

technology (tek nol′ ə jē) The use of science to solve problems. People use **technology** every day.

tecnología El uso de la ciencia para resolver problemas. Usamos la **tecnología** todos los días.

thermometer (thər mom′ ə tər) A tool that measures temperature. You can use a **thermometer** to measure how hot or cold something is.

termómetro Instrumento para medir la temperatura. Puedes usar un **termómetro** para medir cuán caliente o cuán frío está algo.

tool (tül) Something that is used to do work. Some **tools** are used to observe.

instrumento Algo que se usa para hacer trabajo. Algunos **instrumentos** se usan para observar.

volume (vol′ yəm) The amount of space matter takes up. You can use a measuring cup to measure the **volume** of liquids.

volumen Cantidad de espacio que ocupa la materia. Puedes usar una taza de medir para medir el **volumen** de un líquido.

weathering (weᴛH′ ər ing)) When water, ice, or wind breaks down rocks. **Weathering** can change the shape, size, and color of rocks.

meteorización Cuando el agua, el hielo o el viento rompe las rocas. La **meteorización** puede cambiar la forma, el tamaño y el color de las rocas.

Index

Credits

Staff Credits

The people who made up the Interactive Science team—representing composition services, core design digital and multimedia production services, digital product development, editorial, editorial services, manufacturing, and production—are listed below.

Geri Amani, Alisa Anderson, Jose Arrendondo, Amy Austin, David Bailis, Scott Baker, Lindsay Bellino, Jennifer Berry, Charlie Bink, Bridget Binstock, Holly Blessen, Robin Bobo, Craig Bottomley, Jim Brady, Laura Brancky, Chris Budzisz, Odette Calderon, Mary Chingwa, Caroline Chung, Kier Cline, Brandon Cole, Mitch Coulter, AnnMarie Coyne, Fran Curran, Dana Damiano, Michael Di Maria, Nancy Duffner, Susan Falcon, Amanda Ferguson, David Gall, Mark Geyer, Amy Goodwin, Gerardine Griffin, Chris Haggerty, Margaret Hall, Laura Hancko, Autumn Hickenlooper, Guy Huff, George Jacobson, Marian Jones, Abigail Jungreis, Kathi Kalina, Chris Kammer, Sheila Kanitsch, Alyse Kondrat, Mary Kramer, Thea Limpus, Dominique Mariano, Lori McGuire, Melinda Medina, Angelina Mendez, Claudi Mimo, John Moore, Kevin Mork, Chris Niemyjski, Phoebe Novak, Anthony Nuccio, Jeff Osier, Rachel Pancare, Dorothy Preston, Charlene Rimsa, Rebecca Roberts, Camille Salerno, Manuel Sanchez, Carol Schmitz, Amanda Seldera, Jeannine Shelton El, Geri Shulman, Greg Sorenson, Samantha Sparkman, Mindy Spelius, Karen Stockwell, Dee Sunday, Dennis Tarwood, Jennie Teece, Lois Teesdale, Michaela Tudela, Karen Vuchichevich, Melissa Walker, Tom Wickland, James Yagelski, Tim Yetzina

Illustrations

vi, 3, 55, 57, 61 ©Aleksi Markku/Shutterstock; vii, 63, 111, 113, 117 ©Jens Stolt/Shutterstock; viii, 119, 153, 155, 159 Leonello Calvetti/Getty Images; ix, x, 161, 203, 205, 239, 241, 248 ©James Thew/Shutterstock; 26 Precision Graphics, 51 Precision Graphics, 146 Big Sesh Studios

All other illustrations Chandler Digital Art

Photographs

Photo locators denoted as follows: Top (T), Center (C), Bottom (B), Left (L), Right (R), Background (Bkgd)

COVER: Jamie Hall/Shutterstock

FRONT MATTER
i, ii Jamie Hall/Shutterstock; vi (CR) ©David Trood/Getty Images; vii (CR) SELECT GETTY RF Not Digital Vision; viii (CR) ©Maslov Dmitry/Shutterstock; ix (CR) ©Getty Images/Jupiter Royalty Free; x (CR) Getty Royalty Free; xii ©Clem Haagner/Photo Researchers, Inc.; xiii (TC) Jamie Hall/Shutterstock; (CL) ©National Geographic Image Collection/Alamy Royalty Free, (CR,TL) ©Getty Images/Jupiter Royalty Free, (CR,TR) ©Hemis/

Alamy Inc., (CR,CR) ©Photononstop/SuperStock, Inc., (CR, BL) James Osmond/Alamy Inc., (CR, BR) Mary Clark; xiv (C, BC) ©Danno3/Shutterstock, (C, TL) ©Multiart/Shutterstock, (C, TC) ©Ulrich Mueller/Shutterstock, (C, Bkgd) Corbis, (C, CR) Roger Dixon/©DK Images, (C, TCR) ©2009fotofriends/Shutterstock, (C, BR) ©Evlakhov Valeriy/Shutterstock, (C, CR) ©Randal Sedler/Shutterstock; xv (TR) ©David Trood/©David Trood, (TC) ©3C Stock/Alamy Inc., (B, TC) ©Daboost/Shutterstock, (B, TR) ©hamurishi/Shutterstock, (B, TL) ©Sergey Goruppa/Shutterstock; xvi (CL) ©Dennis Hallinan/Alamy Inc., (CR) ©James P. Blair/Getty Royalty Free, (BCR) ©Jupiterimages/Brand X/Alamy Royalty Free, (BR) ©Maridav/Shutterstock; xx–xxi Tiero/Fotolia;

CHAPTER 1 MATTER
2 (C) ©Margaret Durrance/Photo Researchers, Inc.; 5 ©age fotostock/SuperStock; 17 (CR) ©KimKarpeles/Alamy Images; 23 (BR, BL) Getty Royalty Free; 24 (CR) Jason Young/Fotolia, (B) ©Vlastas/Shutterstock; 28 (BL) ©3C Stock/Alamy Images, (C) David Trood/Getty Images; 30 (TR, TC) ©Nikita Rogul/Shutterstock; 31 (BR) ©Artem Svystun/Shutterstock, (TL) ©NIkita Rogul/Shutterstock, (TC) ©Nikita Rogul/Shutterstock; 36 (T) Jupiter Royalty Free; 38 (TR) ©Craig Tuttle/Corbis; 39 (B) ©Cheryl Casey/Shutterstock, (TR) ©Viktor1/Shutterstock, (CR) Gary Ombler/©DK Images; 40 (TC) Randall Stevens/Shutterstock; 41 (BR) Andy Crawford/DK Images; 42 Blend Images/Image Source; 44 Westpic/Fotolia, (Bkgd) Ken Hurst/Alamy, (TR) JOYCE MARSHALL/MCT/Landov; 45 (B) Visi.stock/Fotolia, (T) Peter Tsai Photography/Alamy; 46 Pics721/Fotolia; 47 Natalia Bratslavsky/Fotolia; 50 (CR) ©boumen&japet/Shutterstock, (Bkgrd) Kasia Nowak/Alamy; 51 (BC) ©David Trood/Getty Images, (TR) ©Kim Karpeles/Alamy Images; 53 (TR) ©Artem Svystun/Shutterstock; (CL) Blend Images/Image Source; 55 (B) ©Margaret Durance/Photo Researchers, Inc., (CBL) ©Nikita Rogul/Shutterstock, (BL) Jupiter Royalty Free; 56 (CL) Getty Royalty Free;

CHAPTER 2 PLANTS AND ANIMALS
62 (Bkgrd) ©Clem Haagner/Photo Researchers, Inc., (L) ©Valueline/Punchstock; 65 (T) ©National Geographic Image Collection/Alamy; 76 (CR) ©DK Images, (T) ©Yuji Sakai/Getty Images; 77 (CR) ©Masterfile Royalty-Free; 80 (T) ©Corbis/Jupiter Royalty Free, (C) ©Sasha Weleber/Getty Royalty Free, (B) Stockbyte/Thinkstock; 81 (CC) Aoo3771/Fotolia, (CR) ©Imagemore Co., Ltd./Alamy, (BC) ©Norberto Mario Lauria/Shutterstock, (TR) ©Sigen Photography/Shutterstock, (TR) ©Tim Scott/Shutterstock, (BR) David Murray/©DK Images, (B) Jupiter Images; 82 (B) ©Digital Vision/Thinkstock, (TR, TC) ©Eric Isselée/Shutterstock; 83 (TL) ©Anat-oli/Shutterstock, (TL) ©Eric Isselée/Shutterstock, (CR) ©Leighton Photography & Imaging/Shutterstock, (TC) ©NIK/Shutterstock, (TR) ©Sascha Burkard/Shutterstock, (BR) ©Vinicius Tupinamba/Shutterstock; 84 (TR) ©Ian Scott/Shutterstock, (B) ©Shane Partridge/iStockphoto; 85 (CR) ©Cathy Keifer/Shutterstock, (BL) ©Eric Isselée/Shutterstock, (TC) ©Martin Pateman/Shutterstock; 86 (BL) ©Brett Stoltz/Shutterstock, (BR) Eric Isselée/Shutterstock;

87 (T) DK Images; 88 (T) Birdiegal/Fotolia; 89 (BR) Tania and Jim Thomson/123RF; 90 (TR) ©Eric Gevaert/Shutterstock, (BR) ©Steve Byland/Shutterstock; 91 (C) ©Igorsky/Shutterstock; 92 (CR, BR) DK Images; 93 (TR) ©lilithlita/Fotolia, (BL) ©Daisy Gilardini/Getty Images, (CL) ©David W. Hamilton/Getty Images, (CR) ©Matt Jeppson/Shutterstock, (CC) ©Mauro Rodrigues/Fotolia, (TL) ©Zoltan Pataki/Shutterstock, (TC) ©Rod Planck/Photo Researchers, Inc.; 94 (T) Getty Digital Vision; 95 (CR) ©Dmitry Deshevykh/Alamy; 96 (C) ©Hemera Technologies/Jupiter Royalty Free; 97 (TR) Getty Royalty Free, (CR) Getty Royalty Free; 98 (BR) ©Michele Falzone/Getty Images, (TR) Getty Royalty Free; 99 (BL) ©Masterfile Royalty-Free, (TL) Thinkstock; 100 (T) ©Joel Sartore/Getty Royalty Free; 101 (CR) ©Ed Reschke/Getty Images; 102 (Bkgrd) ©Grant V. Faint/Getty Royalty Free, (BR) ©John R. MacGregor/Getty Images, (BL) ©Weldon Schloneger/Shutterstock; 103 (CR) B&T Media Group Inc./Shutterstock, (BL) Ryan M. Bolton/Shutterstock; 106 (R) ©Francois Gohier/Photo Researchers, Inc.; 107 (BC) Dmitry Deshevykh/Alamy, (TR) ©Masterfile Royalty-Free, (CL) ©Zoltan Pataki/Shutterstock, (TL) ©Shane Partridge/iStockphoto; 109 (T) ©Grant V. Faint/Getty Royalty Free, (B) ©John R. MacGregor/Getty Images, (C) B&T Media Group Inc/Shutterstock; 111 (T) ©Yuji Sakai/Getty Royalty Free, ©Eric Isselée/Shutterstock, Birdiegal/Fotolia, Getty Royalty Free, (B) ©Grant V. Faint/Getty Royalty Free; 112 (TR) Derek Hall/©DK Images; 113 (CR) ©Frank Lukasseck/Getty Royalty Free, (CL) ©Jorg Greuel/Getty Royalty Free, (CC) ©Purestock/Getty Royalty Free;

CHAPTER 3 EARTH'S MATERIALS

118 (C) Ralph Lee Hopkins/National Geographic/Getty Images; 121 (BR) Tomasz Zajda/Fotolia, (TR) ©Rob Byron/Shutterstock; 132 (T) ©Andy Z./Shutterstock, (B) Leksele/Shutterstock; 133 (CR) James Stevenson/Donks Models/©DK Images; 134 (C) ©Brand X Pictures/Getty Images, (B) ©Chris Sattlberger/Getty Images, (T) ©Jupiterimages/Thinkstock, (CC) ©Mike Norton/Shutterstock; 136 (BR) ©Constantine Androsoff/Shutterstock, (TR) ©Nikolay Okhitin/Shutterstock; 137 (BL) ©Imagix/Shutterstock, (TL) Thinkstock; 138 (T) ©Dennis Hallinan/Alamy Images; 139 (T) ©James P. Blair/Getty Images, (CR) ©Jupiterimages/Brand X/Alamy, (BR) ©Maridav/Shutterstock; 140 (L) ©Lee Prince/Shutterstock, (R) Mike Doukas/U.S.Geological Survey; 141 (R) James Schwabel/Alamy Images, (L) Thinkstock; 142 (B) "SambaPhoto/Eduardo Queiroga-Lumiar/GettyImages, (CL) Jose Gil/Fotolia; 143 (B) "Robert Harding Picture Library Ltd/Alamy Images, (TR) Jupiter Images; 144 (TR, TC) Colin Keates/Courtesy of the Natural History Museum, London/©DK Images; 145 (TC) Bastos/Fotolia, (CR) Stephan Schneider/Fotolia, (BR) Colin Keates/Courtesy of the Natural History Museum, London/©DK Images; 147 (TR) ©Falk Kienas/Shutterstock, (B) Andy Crawford/Courtesy of the Royal Tyrrell Museum of Palaeontology, Alberta, Canada/©DK Images; 150 (TR) ©Jupiterimages/Thinkstock, (T, BR) NASA; 151 (BL) Andy Crawford/Courtesy of the Royal Tyrrell Museum of Palaeontology, Alberta, Canada/©DK Images; (LC) Colin Keates/Courtesy of the Natural History Museum, London/©DK Images, (TL) James Schwabel/Alamy Images, (TR) ©Brand X Pictures/Getty Royalty Free, (RC) Imagix/Shutterstock, (BR) Thinkstock; 153 (BC) Ralph Lee Hopkins/National Geographic/Getty Images, (T) © Andy Z./Shutterstock,

(C) ©James P. Blair/Getty Images, Bastos/Fotolia; 154 Jose Gil/Fotolia; 155 (R) Jupiter Images; (C) "Robert Harding Picture Library Ltd/Alamy Images, (L) James Schwabel/Alamy Images; 159 (BR) ©Constantine Androsoff/Shutterstock, (TR) ©Jupiterimages/Thinkstock;

Science, Engineering, and Technology Skills Handbook

PART 1 THE NATURE OF SCIENCE

160 (C) ©Purestock/Getty Royalty Free; 174 (T) ©Stocktrek RF/Getty Images, (B) JSC/NASA; 175 (CR) ©Hemis/Alamy Images; 176 (C) Maxmillian Stock Ltd./Image Bank/Getty Images; 177 (CR) ©AFP/Getty Images, (CL) ©Jeff Greenberg/PhotoEdit, Inc.; 178 (T) ©zerega/Alamy; 179 (CR) ©Peter Dazeley/Getty Images; 180 (C) ©Photononstop/SuperStock; 182 (T) ©Getty Images/Jupiter Royalty Free; 183 (CR) Mary Clark; 187 (B) ©Anderson Ross/Getty Royalty Free; 188 (T) ©Gordon Wiltsie/Getty Images; 189 (CR) ©Getty Images/Jupiter Royalty Free; 192 (T) ©Andreas Scheler/Alamy; 193 (BR) James Osmond/Alamy Inc.; 194 (TR) Colin Keates/Courtesy of the Natural History Museum, London/©DK Images, (CR) DK Images; 198 (R) ©Jet Propulsion Laboratry/NASA Image Exchange, (TR) NASA; 199 (TC) ©Getty Images/Jupiter Royalty Free, (TR) ©Hemis/Alamy Images, (CR) ©Photononstop/SuperStock, (BC) James Osmond/Alamy Images, (BR) Mary Clark; 202 (BR) Thinkstock; 203 (CR) ©Nigel Cattlin/Alamy Inc;

PART 2 TECHNOLOGY AND TOOLS

204 (C) ©Jim Esposito Photography L. L. C./Getty Royalty Free; 207 (T) AlexMaster/Fotolia, (CC) ©Nando/Shutterstock; 218 (B) ©Bernd Mellmann/Alamy Images, (T) Getty Images; 219 (BR) ©Reuters/Corbis; 220 (BCR) ©JG Photography/Alamy, (BR) ©Roy Stevens/Time & Life Pictures/Getty Images, (BL) Dave King/Courtesy of The Science Museum, London/©DK Images, (CL) DK Images, (BCL) Simon Clay/Courtesy of the National Motor Museum, Beaulieu/©DK Images; 221 (TR) ©Paul Maguire/Shutterstock, (BL) Image Courtesy Eastman Kodak Company; 222 (T) ©Mike Flippo/Shutterstock; 223 (CR) ©Peter Gridley/Getty Images; 224 (TR) ©Paul Tearle/Thinkstock; 225 (TR) ©Denis and Yulia Pogostins/Shutterstock; 226 (Bkgrd) ©Evgeny Murtola/Shutterstock; 227 (BR) ©Blend Images/SuperStock; 228 (T) ©Emmanuel Lattes/Alamy Images; 229 (CR) ©Comstock/Thinkstock, (BL) Robert Cocquyt/Fotolia; 230 (TC) ©Massimiliano Leban/iStockphoto, (TR) ©Vstock/Alamy Stock Photo; 231 (CL) James R. Martin/Shutterstock, (TL) ©Comstock/Thinkstock, (CR) ©David Madison/Getty Images, (TR) ©Losevsky Pavel/Shutterstock, (BR) ©Mike Kemp/Getty Images; 232 (CR) ©Frank Cezus/Getty Images, (CL) ©Jason Kasumovic/Shutterstock, (CC) ©PhotoObjects/Thinkstock, (BL) Clive Streeter/©DK Images; 233 (CC) ©Brand X Pictures/Thinkstock, (BR) ©John E. Marriot/Getty Images, (BL) ©David Evison/Shutterstock, (CR) Peter Anderson/©DK Images; 236 (B) ©Arco Images GmbH/Alamy Images, (CR) Clint Keller/The Fort Wayne Journal/©AP Images; 237 (CC) ©Comstock/Thinkstock, (BR) ©Peter Gridley/Getty Images, (CR) ©Reuters/Corbis, (TR) Getty Images; 239 (BL)©Comstock/Thinkstock, (CB) ©Jim Esposito Photography L. L. C./Getty Royalty Free,